Why WORSHIP?

Why WORSHIP?

Understanding the Origin, Relevance and Impact of Your Access to God's Presence

NGINA L. THOMAS

WHY WORSHIP?

Printed in the United States of America

Editor: Sharp Editorial, LLC

At the word of the Lord, entirely yielded to His grace this book was birthed.

From the depth, tribulation, and triumphs endured over more than two decades of walking with God, I present to you "Why Worship?"

May the truths and the Truth scripted in these pages provoke a great well of refreshing in you. May your eyes be opened beyond your expectations and may you run into the bosom of the Father with fire in your feet from this moment forward.

The presence of God is your safe place. Rest well here.

TABLE OF CONTENTS

INTRODUCTION

The Word of God contains the mind, heart, will, strategy, and synchronization of God in written form. The scriptures reveal His plan, person, purpose, and ideology critical to our understanding of His nature. If God's heart were to melt and all of its substance be converted into the form of musical notes, that substance would "sing" the scriptures from the beginning to its end. If His heart were to melt into liquid material, it would overflow endless oceans to be named "The Inspired Word of God."

Although many waste time debating the relevance of the Word surrounding the subject of translation and/or transliteration, what we must keep at the forefront of our minds is that the scriptures were just as inspired as His creation. What has been compiled into what we call the Bible (I most commonly refer to as the Word of God) is intentional. The scriptures testify of themselves, saying that many more acts could be accounted for that exist in books not included in the Bible. Even the gospel of John tells us plainly that Jesus performs many other acts that the pages of all books in the world could not contain (John 21:25). There are many more details to Christ's walk on the earth that no book, single or multiple, could host the full content of His life. **1 Kings 14:18,29, 1 Kings 15:7,23 1 Kings 16:20.

2 Peter 1:20-21 (NKJV) —

> "[Yet] first [you must] understand this, that no prophecy of Scripture is [a matter] of any personal or private or special interpretation (loosening, solving). For no prophecy ever originated because some man willed it [to do so—it never came by human impulse], but men spoke from God who were borne along (moved and impelled) by the Holy Spirit."

The Bible includes a compilation of historical events in the context of God's sovereign and providential rule on earth that He created for a people whom He created for Himself. The intent of the Word is to reveal to us Christ Jesus, the Son of God as Redeemer, Savior, Lord, Intercessor, and The Way (which is what Christianity was called in the Bible) *Acts 19:23. The utterances of men are those of the prophets or men, women, and/or angels to and through whom the Lord has spoken. The supernatural events are actual and have withstood historical scrutiny from all who have contended the validity of the scriptures. The Word of God is sure, true, tried, settled, and most highly honored, even by the Lord God Himself.

God esteems His Word above His name. I will never fully understand the depth of the nature of a God that would decide such an order but what I can whisper by way of His wind (inspiration) is that God's Word is His internal disposition expressed for man's sake. If God did not or does not speak, then we, His creation, have no instruction to live by; we'd have no form or order of any kind. Without the Word of God, the world could have remained void and formless. God the Father is seated far above the heavens. He is eternal and holds all power in His hands. The Word of God is the vehicle or vessel by which that power descends.

Hebrews 11:3 (NKJV) —

> *"By faith, we understand that the worlds were framed by the word of God..."*

His name is great and greatly to be praised; however, if all of what had been created by His Word remained a secret because of His silence, then His heart and mind for the world could not be revealed. God spoke every item in and around the universe into existence by the breath of His mouth. Imagine if He chose to remain silent and the beautiful world in which we live remained a mystery. Where would we be? The release of His Word not only lends credibility to His identity, but it lays the framework for ours. God is our source. His eternal existence is the origin of our origin, and we can only be because He exists in us. This protocol came by way of the Word.

By virtue of His existence, God is a ruler, yet His Word makes His rule have an impact. A king can be a king as long as he is in a crowned position of power and authority, but a king that makes no decrees has no lasting impact. Without the spoken word of a ruler, nothing is established except the reign fulfilled during his lifetime. There is no tenure to his rule without a decree evoking change or order. The impact of His reign is manifested with words.

Ecclesiastes 8:4 (NKJV) —

"Where the word of a king is, there is power."

God's way does not follow the pattern of an earthly royal; instead, royalty follows its pattern after our Sovereign Ruler seated far above the heavens. And this God esteems His Word above His name because, without His Word, His reign would have less impact.

This book is about worship; however, if you do not value the Word, you will undoubtedly misinterpret the subject of worship. To become a worshipper, the Word of God must first come alive in you. One is not without the other. You cannot be a worshipper and deny the Word of God as true. Likewise, you cannot proclaim to be a disciple of the Word yet in no way worship. To understand worship, you must believe that God exists and that He rules.

To understand and live in a place of worship, you must believe that Christ Jesus, the Son of God, was sent to the earth in the form of a seed planted in the womb of a virgin to be born into mankind to re-present mankind back to the Father. Because of Adam's sin in the garden, all became sinners and separated from God. One man committed an offense that destroyed his inherent relationship with the Father. Jesus, the second Man, committed to the plan that reversed it all, reconciling or rejoining us back to our rightful place in God. **Romans 5:19, 1 Corinthians 15:22.

Salvation is your entry point to worship, and I would be remiss to assume you have received salvation simply because you selected this book. If you are saved, great! This book will enhance your understanding of the idea of worship in a major way. If you have yet to receive salvation and truly seek the truth, find your new home in Christ and His kingdom and pray this prayer aloud:

> *Father, in the name of Jesus, I believe that You are God and the only eternal One. I believe that You are triune in being and You, Father, Son, and Holy Spirit, are One. By faith, I receive the salvation that comes because of Your love. Your Word decrees that if I confess with my mouth and believe in my heart that Christ Jesus the Lord came to earth as man, to become my sin, to take my sin to the grave and be resurrected by Your glory, that I would be saved. By faith, I believe that Christ has ascended back into glory and is seated at Your right hand, making intercession for me. By faith, I understand that because I am now made alive in Christ and that Your Holy Spirit has now come to abide in me that You are with me always. You promise to lead me and guide me, and I confess that I will follow You. Father, receive my repentance as an offering as I receive salvation as a gift of Your love. In Jesus' name, Amen.*

Now that we're all in the kingdom and born of Christ's Spirit, let's further understand this phenomenon called worship.

Chapter One

APPROACHING THE SUBJECT

I agree with many scholars that the proper approach to studying terminology found in scripture is by using what is called the "Law of First Mentions." Applying this study strategy, one will find that the first place a term appears in scripture indicates its most essential meaning. In other words, understanding the full context of a word or biblical concept allows the student to grasp God's heart on the matter. Keep in mind that scripture came to man to hear and scribe by the inspiration of Holy Spirit and requires Holy Spirit to understand. Without Him guiding our understanding, we will land in error, which has plagued the belief system of far too many people. For the believer, truth cannot be redefined. Our standard is not of any man's opinion nor our own; rather, the foundation of the truth that makes us free is found in Christ and with good reason.

John 16:13 (KJV) —

> "Howbeit when he, the Spirit of truth, is come, he will guide you into all truth: for he shall not speak of himself; but whatsoever he shall hear, that shall he speak: and he will shew you things to come."

In Hebrew, the word "guide" in John 16:13 is [hodēgeō], pronounced [hod-ayg-eh'-oto], which means to show the way (literally or figuratively [teach]); guide, lead. The student of the Word is dependent on the teacher who the scriptures identify as Holy Spirit, the Person of God in Spirit. I recall a time I yelled at God for not showing me who He was sooner than the day I learned how much He loved me. At church, while I was in prison, I was watching the reenactment of the crucifixion and what hit me like a lightning bolt disinfected me from the rejection that plagued my heart for many years before that moment occurred. In what seemed like an instant, discerning the literal body of Jesus being bruised and beaten for me, I *knew* the love of God for me. It was as if a ball of fire had come down from heaven, planting itself in my heart only to reveal this amazing love I knew to be personally applied to me. With lifted hands and my body bowed down, I travailed out (because this was not just a cry), "Thank You, Father" in such thunder that I'm sure interrupted the worship in heaven. From my heart to His ears was the sound of gratitude for what I learned in a literal moment. In the same tears, what may have been minutes later, I yelled out with my hands still raised, "Why didn't You tell me this sooner? Why would You allow me to live all these years without knowing You this way? Why did You allow me to suffer inside by not knowing You, Father?!" His answer was simple yet extremely powerful. It was one I will never forget. He said to me, "You did not come to Me to discover Who I am. You went to men who do not know Me to discover who I am. You would have never found Me there."

He nailed it.

I grew up in the Islamic faith and later found myself mesmerized by the teachings of Elijah Muhammad and other strong pro-Black leaders whose lessons and messages only further promoted what I felt was the actual truth, which was that Jesus was just a prophet. According to Islamic teachings, that was not a dig to minimize the significance of Jesus. The teachings of the Quran and other religious materials believed it to be of honorable mention to put great men of faith on the same pedestal as Jesus. I had no reason to believe anything more of Him until I was later introduced to truth.

There is a difference between the truth and truth. No other man, man's opinion, ideology, theology, philosophy, cultural reality, or literal history can lead us to truth in God's way. The truth, as in literal or factual reality, is in our history, but our history does not point us to biblical truth. For the believer, truth is found in Jesus Christ, the target of spirit-inspired revelation.

Worship will point you to Christ and the revelation of Christ will provoke you to worship.

John 16:14-15 (KJV) —

> "He shall glorify me: for he shall receive of mine, and shall shew it unto you. All things that the Father hath are mine: therefore said I, that he shall take of mine, and shall shew it unto you."

We come to the saving knowledge of Jesus Christ by way of Holy Spirit who leads and guides us into truth concerning Christ throughout the scriptures from the first to the last book.

As we delve into what I believe is a subject matter most paramount to the life of every believer (and non-believer), I want you to posture your heart to hear God in all to be revealed in the pages your eyes will scroll. Christ is our Light and our Life. His Words are spirit, and they are alive which means no interpretation, revelation, rhema, or written word is outdated.

1 Corinthians 12:3 (NKJV) —

> "Wherefore I give you to understand, that no man speaking by the Spirit of God calleth Jesus accursed: and that no man can say that Jesus is the Lord, but by the Holy Ghost."

In fact, it isn't the preacher or evangelist that introduces us to Christ; rather, it is the Holy Ghost, Christ's Spirit who reveals truth concerning Him.

This revelation along with our acceptance of what is revealed is what provokes the confession of faith leading to salvation. This confession led to our induction into the kingdom of God, the place of God's domain, where we now access, exercise, and experience the impact of His power. How did we get here? By the truth revealed to our spirits by the Spirit of God. It will take our leaning into the same voice that sent truth our way to further reveal truth.

1 Corinthians 2:14 (NKJV) —

> *"But the natural man receiveth not the things of the Spirit of God: for they are foolishness unto him: neither can he know them, because they are spiritually discerned."*

I am not speaking to your natural man. The greatest benefit of worship only serves your outer man as a result of what is done in the hidden realms and your heart. I am speaking to your spirit. The words of life shared in this book will do more than appease your eyes and understanding. You will walk stronger because of the deposit your spirit man receives, and your eyes will be enlightened beyond your natural understanding of the words on this page. As you prepare to hear, an opening is taking place and you will hear what the Spirit of God is saying specifically to you regarding your heart of worship. The impartation received will impact your worship to such a degree that not only will God begin to open Himself up to you in a mighty way by showing you more of His hand and His heart, but your understanding and experience in His presence will open wide; as you worship, you will give birth to dimensions of newness that He has had in store for you for many seasons past.

I even sense that as you begin to walk deeper in Him, seeking His face and heart, answers will continually unfold to unlock secret after secret regarding your destiny. Others will find you to be their wellspring of wisdom because you will grow in capacity to hear for those around you, including your family, friends, and colleagues. Wisdom comes to those who seek the One who is all-wise and all-knowing. This portal of access, favor, and divine revelation is opening to you as you seek the Lord by way of what is called worship. You will inherit a life of light, and darkness will only remain around you if you stay silent. But I decree that as you begin to lift your head with the perspective that you will gain through worship, your renewed aerial view will cause you to not only forget those things which are behind (i.e., past pains, hurts, traumas, dead ends, closed doors, relationship woes, etc.) but that you will inherit a newness of life in your eyes. Your eyes will be filled with light, and you will see life ahead and around you with a clear lens. It will be up to you to remain in this place and to know that you never have to leave a life of worship to live a natural life. In fact, you will invite the atmosphere that worship brings into every area, and you will live differently.

Chapter Two

WHAT IS WORSHIP? DEFINED BY THE LAW OF FIRST MENTIONS

The Law of First Mentions leads us to Genesis 22, where Abraham, known as our father in the faith, is instructed by the Lord to offer his own son as a sacrifice unto God. It sounds inhumane and void of God's character, but His instruction was only a test.

Without wavering, Abraham obeyed God. This offering was considered an act of worship and notes the first of its kind in scripture. In case you are unfamiliar with this account, and before getting caught up or turned off at what God asked him for, know that there is more to the story.

Worship is an act of obedience. It involves presenting an acceptable offering unto God. In its simplicity, to worship is to obey God. In a more complex sense, to worship is to trust God with an unwavering faith that will grant you peace in offering whatever the Lord requires of you. What you grasp from this chapter will strengthen your lifestyle worship.

Genesis 22:1-5 (KJV) —

"And it came to pass after these things, that God did tempt Abraham, and said unto him, Abraham: and he said, Behold, here I am. And he said, Take now thy son, thine only son Isaac, whom thou lovest, and get thee into the land of Moriah; and offer him there for a burnt offering upon one of the mountains which I will tell thee of. And Abraham rose up early in the morning, and saddled his ass, and took two of his young men with him, and Isaac his son, and clave the wood for the burnt offering, and rose up, and went unto the place of which God had told him. Then on the third day Abraham lifted up his eyes, and saw the place afar off. And Abraham said unto his young men, Abide ye here with the ass; and I and the lad will go yonder and worship, and come again to you."

Let's dissect this verse by verse.

"And it came to pass after these things, that God did tempt Abraham, and said unto him, Abraham: and he said, Behold, here I am."

The call to worship came through testing "after these things." The "things" preceding this monumental moment of Abraham's life and transition into promise indicate a series of events behind this particular call to worship. The history of Abraham's relationship with God and God's relationship with Abraham helps us to understand the mind of God regarding His instruction. Abraham's relationship with God did not begin in this verse; rather, Abrahams's relationship with God began with an encounter. Before God asks you for worship, He will offer you an encounter.

Genesis 22:12 (NKJV) —

"The Lord had said to Abram, 'Leave your native country, your relatives, and your father's family, and go to the land that I will show you.'"

God did not wait for Abram to follow Him, serve Him, pray to Him, or worship Him before He called Abraham (formerly called Abram) into promise. There was nothing about Abraham's life that convinced God that he was deserving to be called into what God had in store for him. Abraham did not prepare himself for his introduction to God. On the contrary, the Lord introduced Himself to Abram in a manner that interrupted his life.

God encountered Abram right where he was, which was in a land and amid a culture caught up in idolatrous worship. Abram lived a life filled with the common practices of paganism and Baal worship. His original forms of worship were all considered detestable, yet none of this deterred the Lord from calling out Abram. What the Lord had prepared for Abraham preceded his response and subsequent obedience. Every promise that was set ahead of Abram's current living condition had already been established. His way into unearned, unqualified destiny was obedience to the voice that called him out of familiarity. While enjoying the comfort of his former lifestyle, the Lord God met him with an encounter that would lead Abram right into his set future in mind.

Do you know that it was while we were dead in sin that Christ died for us, bridging the gap and paving the way for our entry into destiny His way? It was while we surrendered to carnality and were unaware of the darkness in us and around us that He died to save us. God didn't await your yes to His call for you or your yielding to His way to do one single thing for you. Before you knew there was a God that loved you, He made a way for you.

Abraham's relationship with God began the moment he was called, not when he was asked for an offering. Let the patterns of God revealed in His Word help you to gauge His heart and His way.

God does not initiate a relationship with us by giving instructions. God is not a religious ruler setting laws and ordinances before us that require our blind faith or walk of perfection. He does not approve our access to Him by our sinlessness. That is why I dislike religion which opposes and does great harm by diminishing the truth of the gospel. Religion reminds you of the law exposing your unrighteousness and deems you unfit for God without perfection or sinless living. The gospel of the kingdom promotes Christ's sacrifice on behalf of the sinfulness that renders you clean, accepted, and perfected forever.

Hebrews 10:14 (NKJV) —

> *"For by one offering He has perfected forever those who are being sanctified."*

I see why Jesus rebuked the religious. On the contrary, God initiates a relationship with man by His giving of Himself. His endless love for us dictates His pursuit of us. God is not the author of religion repelled by man's frailty and flesh nature; instead, He is the author of relationship that covers our frailty with the covenant.

It was after sequential events or encounters with Abraham that God decided to test him. What we can learn from this is that testing follows equipping. I remember being in a hair-coloring class some years ago. We had live models and no mannequins, just our master teacher with products and tools. It was a blonding class. Naturally, every model attending had volunteered to be colored blonde. Our instructor led us in the formulation of the lightener; however, when it came for its application, little to no instruction was given. We were left to apply the formula based on our knowledge and skill, although we all came as students to learn. Unaware that coloring hair to this level of blonde required a particular application pattern, the instructor took notice of our error and inserted a correction that came after our mistake was made. We had already begun to apply the product based on our former knowledge. We were sent to rinse the product out of the model's hair and reapply it. Having noticed our frustration, the instructor calmly said what I adamantly believe is false: "To learn to do some things right, you have to first do it wrong." Wanting to remain respectful, I kept this thought to myself: "To learn to do things right, we need to be taught the correct way." The time she afforded us to apply the product without leadership was intentional. The instructor hoped to expose our weaknesses through a test. We had been prematurely tested yet were too underdeveloped to pass. Final exams are given to students once a semester has come to an end, not during the orientation. A driver exam takes place after classes are taken, not when a permit is approved.

Usually, the test comes after the building. It is after they build the car that they test it. After they build the toy, they test it. After they build the machine, they test it. No architect or builder of homes builds for failure. They build for endurance. Mechanical failures are accidental and reveal which areas require more attention. The test comes to affirm, not to destroy. Before God tests you, He equips you to endure.

Abram was 75 years old when the Lord called him and 100 years old when Isaac was born. Historians discuss the age of Isaac being between five and 36 years old when he was bound by his father to be sacrificed as an offering. For the sake of our discussion, let's take the low end and say Isaac was five years old at the time mentioned in our text. That means it was ten chapters and a minimum of 30 years later that Abraham was presented with a test. Over more than two decades of fellowship and since he was initially called, God established a track record for a man entirely unfamiliar with His way. Time and time again, God met with Abraham, personally and publicly, all of which allowed Abraham time to learn God's way. From Genesis 12 and on, we see God speaking His promises, revealing His plans, performing miracles, pardoning sin, making ways of escape, giving him victory, providing wealth and riches, and meeting every need Abraham could have. After the training and equipping came the testing.

It is the pattern of God to first show Himself to us to establish His identity in our hearts. Then, He asks for worship. You will note this pattern in all of scripture from the Old Testament into the New Testament. God shows us who He is and then He asks us for worship. Our walk with God should mirror this pattern. First, He is revealed. After the revealing comes our acknowledgment which leads us to follow. As we follow, we are discipled. As we are discipled, we are tested.

Genesis 22:2 (KJV) —

> *"And he said, Take now thy son, thine only son Isaac, whom thou lovest, and get thee into the land of Moriah; and offer him there for a burnt offering upon one of the mountains which I will tell thee of."*

God called Isaac Abraham's only son, fully aware that Ishmael was born first (Genesis 16). Note that God only considers what is birthed out of promise an acceptable sacrifice. To remedy her barrenness, Sarah offered her maid to her husband. Sarah wanted a son and could not stand the idea of being considered infertile or incapable of giving birth. In those days, to be barren or without children was worse than being poor and was a sign of God's restrained blessing, punishment, or curse. To produce what God said would come supernaturally, Sarah chose to compromise by mothering a child born out of another woman's womb. Her decision to do this was not God's plan for how Isaac would come. Sarah decided what she thought was best for them while God had decided what would serve the destiny of many generations to follow. Her decision to do this appeased her issue of barrenness for a moment but later came back to haunt her. What her decision did not do was provoke the Lord to reassign His promise to another:

Genesis 17:15-16 (NKJV) —

> *"Then God said to Abraham, 'As for Sarai your wife, you shall not call her name Sarai, but Sarah shall be her name. And I will bless her and also give you a son by her; then I will bless her, and she shall be a mother of nations; kings of peoples shall be from her.'"*

What the Lord would give birth to would come supernaturally. He did not curse Sarai with barrenness. Instead, He preserved her womb for an appointed time. The son that God would bless with covenant would come from Sarah's own body, not the womb of her maid. The Lord does not need us to borrow blessings from others. Whom the Lord will bless, He will provide. What was birthed out of compromise, carnality, doubt, and fear was not able to replace the perfect plan of God regarding how He intended to create legacy and generational blessing from this family.

As it was with Abraham, so it is for you. No plan of yours will replace God's perfect Will for your life. Usually, His promises are released to you during personal times of fellowship, preaching, or prophetic release. This is why it is imperative to remain in a posture to hear God, whether with personal study and time spent reading the Word or attending a faith-filled, accurately teaching church.

Sarah's participation was essential, yet her impatience would not contaminate the perfection of God's intention. The promise of God, not our desire, determines the course of His actions. Ishmael was blessed for generations to come yet his blessing did not displace what was assigned to Isaac.

God does not consider compromise.

What is clear is that despite what sounds like an incredulous idea, Abraham's response to God was immediate. I don't want to get ahead of myself and teach this out of order, but I will mention that offering up human sacrifice was one of the detestable practices God opposed in the Book of Leviticus. I wondered why the Lord, whose nature and way do not change, would ask such a thing of Abraham. I don't want anyone confused by this for the story does not end here. It was a test. God was testing Abraham's obedience to follow without reservation.

God's nature is untaintable (uncompromising, without blemish, perfect) and His ways are high and holy. Everything He does is driven by holy intention. The Lord did not want Abraham's son. He wanted Abraham's heart. This admonition was given to reveal what was in Abraham's heart, to test his level of trust toward God. Not only has this type of testing revealed the heart of Abraham, but it also revealed the heart of God. The Lord will walk with us, speak with us, provide for us, and make ways for us, but He will also test our hearts in a call to worship. Furthermore, the scripture reveals that He will always provide what God is to require of us. Understanding His nature and accepting that His way is holy and without fault, obedience to His voice should always follow our hearing of Him. It was obedience that gave way to Abraham's offering of Isaac. Although sacrificial offering is a part of our lives of worship, obedience is supreme.

1 Samuel 15:22 (NIV) —

> "But Samuel replied: 'Does the Lord delight in burnt offerings and sacrifices as much as in obeying the Lord? To obey is better than sacrifice, and to heed is better than the fat of rams.'"

Will you offer what you love most? Will you offer what God promised and provided even if it leaves you wanting? Will you offer what hurts the most to give? Will you offer the thing you've waited for the longest to come? Those are relevant challenges that determine the course of our actions and how hard we follow after God. Worship requires our obedience which leads us to encounter what we offer. We hear, we follow, we encounter, and we obey. This describes the life of the worshipper who walks with God.

Worship is not just obedience; worship is a form of obedience and yielding to God that further reveals His nature, substantiating our trust.

Hebrews 11:17-19 (NKJV) —

> "By faith Abraham, when he was tried, offered up Isaac: and he that had received the promises offered up his only begotten son, Of whom it was said, That in Isaac shall thy seed be called: Accounting that God

was able to raise him up, even from the dead; from whence also he received him in a figure."

This man who walked by faith was fully convinced that if this painful exchange was required, this same God could raise Him from the dead. Abraham knew his God! The death and resurrection of Christ did not take place for thousands of years, yet what Abraham learned of God became the revelation to which he yielded his entire life. Confidence in God without compromise will draw God's attention to you.

Listen to what Abraham told Isaac just before wrapping him up and laying his body on the wood.

Genesis 22:8 (NKJV) —

"And Abraham said, My son, God will provide for Himself the lamb for a burnt offering."

What did Abraham discern that assured him that a sacrifice would be provided? What could he have known of God that gave him the type of confidence moving forward that showed no hesitation? The atoning quality of a lamb for the offering was not yet taught. Abraham had a revelation.

This act of worship was such an enormous display of hope, faith, and trust that I don't believe Abraham moved at a slower pace than normal. It was a three-day journey from where he migrated after leaving Haran, the land of his fathers, and Mount Moriah, the place he was sent to sacrifice. If any other detail were relevant to our reading, it would have been printed within the context of this passage of scripture. What God wants us to gather is that the evidence of our faith and following after Him results in worship without worry and provision for every promise.

There is no hesitation in the cadence of this great man of faith, and when we grow to know God as Abraham did, there should be no delay in ours.

Genesis 22:11 (NKJV) —

> *"But the angel of the Lord called out to him from heaven and said, 'Abraham, Abraham!' So he said, 'Here I am.'"*

Can we take a moment to acknowledge that another characteristic of worship is that it positions you to hear from heaven? Your life on earth no longer separates you from the voice of God and should therefore not separate you from the will of God. There was no distance between the man of faith and the God that rewards those that walk in faith.

Here is the remainder of this story in verse 12.

> *"And He said, 'Do not lay your hands on the lad, or do anything to him; for now I know that you fear God, since you have not withheld your son, your only son, from Me.'"*

Abrahams's obedience marked this moment. His obedience displayed a level of maturity expected of God at this moment. Abraham's learning of God is one thing, but it was what God now knew about Abraham that accelerated his promotion into promise. "For *now* I know that you fear God" was the Lord's response to Abraham's honor of the word of instruction.

Worship is the lifestyle of those that fear the Lord. Our worship is evidence of our reverence. Abraham grew accustomed to hearing and obeying the voice of the Lord, and God knew Abraham was mature enough in hearing to follow Him to this degree. I sincerely believe that had it taken Abraham several times of testing to get here, he would not have been promoted without passing. All that God has for you will be released after times of testing essential to your life of worship. Encounter with God is not singular but progressive and continual. He wants you prepared for your inheritance; oftentimes, your maturity will be tested in unseemly ways.

In the time of fellowship, Abraham's familiarity with the Father anchored him enough to trust God. He knew that what is born of a God-seed cannot die. In the promise is planted an eternal factor called the perfect plan of God.

Worship continually reveals the perfect plan of God. A lifestyle of worship is our contribution to God's covenant unfolding in our lives. Worship displays our acknowledgment of God as One who is near and one who can sustain us regardless of what life presents us. To worship, we must hear God's voice and know enough about His ways that lead us to yield and surrender.

For years, I have defined worship as "the response man offers to the God we see." I have confessed for years that worship saved my life. True encounter for me became the foundation that fueled my pursuit of God to this day. He encountered me when I had nothing to give; I had practiced sin so long that I became a professional. Like it was with Abraham, every encounter I had with God taught me something, and what I learned of Him led me to deeper levels of obedience. As I continued to experience Him, I continued to grow in sensitivity to His presence and heart that further revealed His love.

As was the case with Abraham, trust became easier for me after encounter. Did I see Him with my eyes? No. I experienced Him in ways more tangible than my natural senses would allow. Through fellowship, which is a lifestyle of worship, the Lord revealed Himself to me as well as me to me in ways that made me appropriate my weakness with submission and surrender. What I learned of God 20 years ago is what I am governed by now. I can trust God with my surrender.

Chapter Three

THE ORIGIN OF WORSHIP

When and where did true worship begin? With so many voices leading and so many choices, how can we know who or what is true? Aren't there many ways to get to God and shouldn't any way we find lead us to the same place? Who really defines worship anyway? Is it God or man? How and who did men worship before they worshipped God? Do a variety of cultures have varying expressions of worship? Aren't they all valid? Who determines that one form of worship is more acceptable while another is denied?

Those questions left unanswered will have some seekers in indecision, some left to follow heresy while others simply follow blindly led by grandma's influence. Truth revealed is the intention of God in all areas of our seeking, however, from God's perspective, blind obedience leading to salvation does not equate to faith. I would dare say until you are sure of a revelation of Christ leading to your salvation, you may be better off remaining as you were. Lacking the ammunition that accompanies the revelation will leave you powerless in the field of spiritual attack and you will become easy prey for the enemy if you are not grounded in faith. When it comes to your submission to salvation, you need to be sure and know Who you are following.

If you are unsure as to who lordship is attributed to, you will not follow God with conviction. Your life will merely mimic believers as opposed to producing authentic fruit of your own. You would be among the many that have a form of godliness but deny the power thereof (2 Timothy 3:5). To access His power, a revelation of Christ is required, and even more than that is the confession following the revelation. The kingdom of God, or salvation, comes to you because of your confession of faith.

Romans 10:9-10 (NLT) —

> "If you openly declare that Jesus is Lord and believe in your heart that God raised him from the dead, you will be saved. For it is by believing in your heart that you are made right with God, and it is by openly declaring your faith that you are saved."

The confession of faith comes to you by way of revealed knowledge from the Spirit of God Himself.

1 Corinthians 12:3 (AMP) —

> "Therefore I want you to know that no one speaking by the [power and influence of the] Spirit of God can say, 'Jesus be cursed,' and no one can say, 'Jesus is [my] Lord,' except by [the power and influence of] the Holy Spirit."

Let's look at Peter's confession that got the Lord's attention in Matthew 16:13-16 (KJV) —

> "When Jesus came into the coasts of Caesarea Philippi, he asked his disciples, saying, Whom do men say that I the Son of man am? And they said, Some say that thou art John the Baptist: some, Elias; and others, Jeremias, or one of the prophets. He saith unto them, But whom say ye that I am? And Simon Peter answered and said, Thou art the Christ, the Son of the living God."

Caesarea Philippi, in many respects, was a lot like the world we live in today as its culture was filled with many mixed beliefs. The influence of Greek and Roman culture abounded here, leading to the erection of many pagan temples and idols commonly raised up and served. Caesarea Philippi was a hodgepodge of different belief systems and religious practices located on a coastal shore where trades were made. Anyone raised under this culture had every right to be confused or submitted to one or several of these so-called gods. So, when Jesus asked Peter, *"But who do you say that I am?"* He was looking for truth amid a culture ingrained in deception and false idol worship. Jesus wanted to see which of those following Him could discern truth amid confusion, and He requires the same of us today. Someone looking to tap into spiritual realities is not limited to the discovery that Christ is Lord.

God will never usurp man's authority or his exercise of free will to decide which way he should go. At the same time, the Lord, who does not change, will not conform to the image of man's choice nor man's conscience. God is the same, then and now. Men can receive revelation concerning who God is and follow truth or man can select his god out of the many choices available. Peter began recounting what the others in the community were saying about Jesus, but Jesus wasn't interested in the false reports of men. He wanted to hear from Peter himself. The Lord requires confession from those that appear faithful to determine if you are faith-filled. Do you agree with Peter?

Matthew 16:16-18 (KJV) —

> *"And Simon Peter answered and said, Thou art the Christ, the Son of the living God. And Jesus answered and said unto him, Blessed art thou, Simon Barjona: for flesh and blood hath not revealed it unto thee, but my Father which is in heaven. And I say also unto thee, That thou art Peter, and upon this rock I will build my church; and the gates of hell shall not prevail against it."*

Jesus called Peter "blessed," which in its Greek context is "makarios," [pronounced mak-ar'-ee-os], which means to be supremely blessed; by extension, fortunate, well off. This revelation was to Peter's fortune or favor. What was revealed, leading Peter to this confession, made him "well off." In other words, this revelation gave Peter an advantage. That favor, fortune, and advantage were called the keys of the kingdom of heaven and granted Peter the power to bring heaven's reality to earth. It is critical to read these scriptures in more of their literal context as offered in the amplified translation below.

Matthew 16:19 (AMP) —

> *"I will give you the keys (authority) of the kingdom of heaven; and whatever you bind [forbid, declare to be improper and unlawful] on earth will have [already] been bound in heaven, and whatever you loose [permit, declare lawful] on earth will have [already] been loosed in heaven."*

(AMPC) —

> *"I will give you the keys of the kingdom of heaven; and whatever you bind (declare to be improper and unlawful) on earth must be what is already bound in heaven; and whatever you loose (declare lawful) on earth must be what is already loosed in heaven."*

With Peter's revelation came the authorization for him to duplicate heaven's order on earth. The confession of faith unlocks realms of power and authority and grants use of what the scriptures call "keys" or access to unlimited power. This is the confession that later became a memorial to his former identity, for it was at this confession that Peter's name was changed. The moment you believe in your heart and confess with your mouth that Jesus the Christ is Lord of all, what happened to Peter happens to you. You now have keys as well as a new name.

What requires revelation is hidden knowledge. It has been the pattern of God to hide His knowledge in mysteries. He does this so that man does not rely on their intellect to understand His ways. His ways and thoughts are higher than ours and much of the understanding we gain that leads to abundant and everlasting life requires spiritual vs. natural understanding.

1 Corinthians 2:14 (AMP) —

> *"But the natural [unbelieving] man does not accept the things [the teachings and revelations] of the Spirit of God, for they are foolishness [absurd and illogical] to him; and he is incapable of understanding them, because they are spiritually discerned and appreciated, [and he is unqualified to judge spiritual matters]."*

The apostle Peter admonishes us to always be ready to give a defense to everyone that asks us a reason for the hope that is in us (1 Peter 3:15). The defense we prepare to give will answer questions of others. The defense I am prepared to offer you now and those who ask why I follow Christ will answer many questions and provide much clarity as we are taught by our Teacher whose name is Holy Spirit.

Worship began in Heaven, not on earth. Before the worlds were framed, there was worship unto God. I want to distinguish the God of the Bible from any other god you may have ever considered in the past or any other god you may be considering now. The God that leads the life of the believer is not self-contrived; He is the only One responsible for creation and the One who upholds it according to Hebrews 1:3 (NKJV) —

> *"Who being the brightness of his glory, and the express image of his person, and upholding all things by the word of his power…"*

John 1:3 (AMP) —

> *"All things were made and came into existence through Him; and without Him not even one thing was made that has come into being."*

(NKJV) —

> "All things were made through Him, and without Him nothing was made that was made."

Isaiah 40:28 declares He is "...the Creator of the ends of the earth..." The prophet Isaiah declares His name as Wonderful, Counselor, Mighty God, Everlasting Father, and Prince of Peace.

Isaiah 9:6 (NKJV) —

> "For unto us a Child is born, Unto us a Son is given; And the government will be upon His shoulder. And His name will be called Wonderful, Counselor, Mighty God, Everlasting Father, Prince of Peace."

He is identified as the "Child" prophesied to be born, and the "Son" prophesied to be given. (To prophesy is to speak in advance by way of the revealing of God.) This prophecy was fulfilled with Mary's virgin birth.

Matthew 1:22-23 (KJV) —

> "Now all this was done, that it might be fulfilled which was spoken of the Lord by the prophet, saying, Behold, a virgin shall be with Child, and shall bring forth a Son, and they shall call his name Emmanuel, which being interpreted is, God with us."

Let's look at Matthew 2:2, and we will pull this thought together.

Matthew 2:1-3 (NKJV) —

> "Now after Jesus was born in Bethlehem of Judea in the days of Herod the king, behold, wise men from the East came to Jerusalem, saying, 'Where is He who has been born King of the Jews? For we have seen His star in the East and have come to worship Him.'"

The Wise Men, also called Magi, observed prophecy fulfilled spoken by Balaam and Daniel in the Old Testament, that a star would appear indicating the Messiah's arrival. When the time came, they also came to worship Him. We will continue working on the text to solidify and ferment in our hearing exactly who God is.

The same God, the Child and Son to come, speaks on behalf of Himself to the nation of Israel saying, "*I am the Lord your God, The Holy One of Israel, your Savior...*" (Isaiah 43:3 NKJV).

In verse 7 of the same chapter, He identifies Himself as the One who gathers us from the ends of the earth, who calls us by His name, who has created us for His glory. This God declares of Himself that He has formed us and made us.

Isaiah 43:7 (NKJV) —

> "*Even every one that is called by my name: for I have created him for my glory, I have formed him; yea, I have made him.*"

We are not an ape's leftovers as the theory of evolution would suggest. We have been created by God Almighty. He further proclaims in Isaiah 43:10-12 (KJV) —

> "*Ye are my witnesses, saith the Lord, and my servant whom I have chosen: that ye may know and believe me, and understand that I am he: before me there was no God formed, neither shall there be after me. I, even I, am the Lord; and beside me there is no savior. I have declared, and have saved, and I have shewed, when there was no strange god among you: therefore ye are my witnesses, saith the Lord, that I am God. Those having experienced the saving power of God called, created and formed for His glory are His very own witnesses. There is something inside of every living being made to acknowledge*

God. At encounter and through continual fellowship yielded vessels acknowledge His reign."

Man, incomparable and finite to God in construction and nature, cannot reconstruct Him in any way. I am amazed at the number of people who have failed calculus class yet believe they possess the intellectual capacity to deconstruct God. He takes the foolish things to confound those believing they are wise. He is not the universe; He created the universe. He is not a magician, nor can He be minimized to just a prophet. He is the Lord God of All, of creation, of Israel, of you, and me. Without receiving the revelation of Him that comes by way of Holy Spirit, as further proven in scripture and evidenced in His creation, we would remain in our former state of perpetual blindness. We come to Him not only blind but blind and bound. Like Abraham, He calls us out of our former state, unaware of our former captivity, into the light He provides. For our blindness, He makes us see and for our shackles, He gives us freedom. Our reasonable response is the reverential fear that induces our life of worship. Our new sight gives us the ability to see God as He is. When we do, we worship.

2 Corinthians 4:4 (NKJV) —

"In whom the god of this world hath blinded the minds of them which believe not, lest the light of the glorious gospel of Christ, who is the image of God, should shine unto them."

He is so merciful, kind, and loving. He does not leave the blind behind. Instead, He calls the blind forward.

Isaiah 43:8-13 (MSG) —

"Get the blind and deaf out here and ready— the blind (though there's nothing wrong with their eyes) and the deaf (though there's nothing wrong with their ears). Then get the other nations out here and ready. Let's see what they have to say about this, how they account for what's

happened. Let them present their expert witnesses and make their case; let them try to convince us what they say is true. 'But you are my witnesses.' God's Decree. 'You're my handpicked servant So that you'll come to know and trust me, understand both that I am and who I am. Previous to me there was no such thing as a god, nor will there be after me. I, yes I, am God. I'm the only Savior there is. I spoke, I saved, I told you what existed long before these upstart gods appeared on the scene. And you know it, you're my witnesses, you're the evidence.' God's Decree. 'Yes, I am God. I've always been God and I always will be God. No one can take anything from me. I make; who can unmake it?'''

The Lord our God is one. He is eternal. He is uncreated. He is seated far above the heavens, and the earth is His footstool. The Lord God is the Judge of all, the Ruler of the nations. He is the King of all kings and the Lord of all lords. There is none like Him, nor any beside Him. He does not share His glory with any other and never will. His seat, name, authority, and position are ranked higher than any form of creation He granted the power to operate for or against Him. Jesus is God and He serves us with His rule that requires and defines the epitome of worship.

Revelations 1:5-8 (KJV) —

"And from Jesus Christ, who is the faithful witness, and the first begotten of the dead, and the prince of the kings of the earth. Unto him that loved us, and washed us from our sins in his own blood, And hath made us kings and priests unto God and his Father; to him be glory and dominion for ever and ever. Amen. Behold, he cometh with clouds; and every eye shall see him, and they also which pierced him: and all kindreds of the earth shall wail because of him. Even so, Amen. I am Alpha and Omega, the beginning and the ending, saith the Lord, which is, and which was, and which is to come, the Almighty."

Jesus is eternal and He is eternity. He is the uncreated Ancient of Days who was before the beginning. God has no origin because He is the God who was and is to come. Jesus is the Word Who became Flesh (John 1:1-2 NKJV) —

> "In the beginning was the Word, and the Word was with God, and the Word was God. The same was in the beginning with God."

Jesus is not just a man that came as natural men do. He came to the earth the same way all of God's promises do—by supernatural intervention. Abraham, being a forerunner, was called to offer his son to mirror God's plan of offering His own Son, Jesus Christ, the Son of the living God. Jesus is not just some man nor is He just some prophet. He is God who became man to be an example of life to man, to be a sacrifice for man, to overcome death for the sins of man, to then carry man to glory where everlasting mercy, forgiveness, and access are granted for all eternity.

John 1:14 (NKJV) —

> "And the Word became flesh and dwelt among us, and we beheld His glory, the glory of the only begotten of the Father full of grace and truth."

Jesus is the only supernaturally relocated person of the triune godhead that, having taken on the form of man for a time, qualifies for our worship. God the Father, God the Son, and God the Holy Spirit—the three expressions/seats/manifestations of God are one according to 1 John 5:7.

In heaven, before the earth gained form and before man was created, planted, and introduced to idols, there was Jesus, the One and true living God; the Author of salvation; the High Priest of our faith; the endless and perfect Creator and Sustainer, seated on the throne surrounded by nothing but worship. Day and night and night and day, the angels, living creatures, and heavenly elders sang and bowed proclaiming Revelation 4:8 (NKJV) —

"Holy, holy, holy, Lord God Almighty Who was and is and is to come!"

Then again, they sang in verse 11 —

"You are worthy, O Lord, to receive glory and honor and power; For You created all things and by Your will they exist and were created."

And the singing continued in Revelation 5:12-13 (NKJV) —

"Saying with a loud voice: 'Worthy is the Lamb who was slain To receive power and riches and wisdom, And strength and honor and glory and blessing!' And every creature which is in heaven and on the earth and under the earth and such as are in the sea, and all that are in them, I heard saying, 'Blessing and honor and glory and power Be to Him who sits on the throne, And to the Lamb, forever and ever!'"

What is the origin of worship? Heaven is the origin of worship. The innermost chamber of the tabernacle, hosting the glory of God, hidden in the days of old now revealed through the coming of Christ is where worship originated, around the throne of God.

Worship first began in the realm of the unseen, and the types of worship engaged in reflected the identity or the form of the spiritual entity being served. Those who reverence God worship Him. Those that look to idols worship them. All worship is not created equal. One would be remiss to attribute true, authentic worship to community or culture because worship was initiated before there was dirt on the ground before continents were formed.

Genesis 8:15-17 (NKJV) —

"Then God spoke to Noah, saying, 'Go out of the ark, you and your wife, and your sons and your sons' wives with you. Bring out with you every living thing of all flesh that is with you: birds and cattle and every

creeping thing that creeps on the earth, so that they may abound on the earth, and be fruitful and multiply on the earth."

We simply cannot attribute true worship to a geographical location or earthly culture because worship from heaven was translated on earth by way of an interpreter of darkness or an interpreter of light. God said to Noah in response to his offering of worship, *"Now go abound in the earth."* The generations that abounded out of Noah and his three sons became the populations migrating to regions later named, filled, and colonized with people we ascribe to each land.

Genesis 9:18-19 (NKJV) —

"Now the sons of Noah who went out of the ark were Shem, Ham, and Japheth. And Ham was the father of Canaan. These three were the sons of Noah, and from these the whole earth was populated."

All created man began in God, were found in Adam, and were preserved in Noah before migration throughout the diaspora. No natural, earthly origin we associate with is man's actual origin. From creation's lens, we all had our beginning in God, having been first born spirit and then made flesh like Jesus. We can therefore only inaccurately ascribe worship to a culture, region, or people. Before there was China, India, Africa, Greece, Haiti, Brazil, Jamaica, the Philippines, etc., and the disseminated influences of worship respective to their cultures, there was worship in heaven from which we derive this phenomenon in its purest form.

When I first got saved, I placed a demand on God to give me insight into His perspective on slavery. I needed to understand His position on the matter. I knew Who I encountered was the real deal, but I held onto the cultural pride preventing me from ingesting the gospel I heard in prior years. My disposition then was the same disposition many Black Americans hold on to now—"We don't want a white man's religion or a white man's God." Studying the Word, I came to the understanding that God was not introduced to slave masters and handed down. God preceded the practice of white slave masters by ions of years. The same lying spirit that authored heresy during the days of the Nephilim authored religion that supported white supremacy. What was presented to Black slaves through white slave masters was not the actual gospel of Jesus Christ but a perverted version supporting the doctrines that supported their evil. God did not hate Black people and did not make whites superior to Black people or any other race. His love is endless for all of mankind. Ham, the son of Noah, who birthed generations into lands such as Africa, committed an awful sin against his father. For Ham's sin, he was cursed to be the lowest of servants to his brothers. This account in its entirety can be found in Genesis 9:18-28. It should by no means be misinterpreted. Followers of Christ have not inherited the God of the white man. We have not exchanged truth to follow the lie gifted to us by oppressors. Jesus is not a blue-eyed white man with flowing blonde hair. We, Black believers of Christ, know Who we worship. We follow after the Ancient of Days, the Uncreated One who created the heavens and the earth. We follow Jesus the Christ, the Son of the Living God, who became flesh for redemption's sake but is not a mere man as some suppose. We are not following slave masters in our practice of faith; we are following God. So many hold onto the idea that how Indigenous Africans worshipped before being sold into slavery was our original form of worship and should not have been lost or exchanged for anything else. Those that believe this will need to sit with discipled, converted Africans who can offer them details of the grossly dark ancestral worship practices in Africa.

We, the believers, distinguish worship of the God of the Bible in the Person of Jesus Christ from the worship of any other god. We do this in accordance with scripture, as the God of the Bible distinguishes Himself and the worship associated with His name. No lower level, low ranking, false idol men have been deceived into believing should gain the attention or obeisance of believers. Spiritual guides, or sources of power drawing our worship, are not created equal. God is eternal and holy which means by virtue of His existence, He is forever in His own category. It is time that believers stop sharing His glory with another by offering praise to graven, or carved images.

Isaiah 42:8 (NKJV) —

> "I am the Lord: that is my name: and my glory will I not give to another, neither my praise to graven images."

Isaiah 42: 5-9 (MSG) —

> "God's Message, the God who created the cosmos, stretched out the skies, laid out the earth and all that grows from it, Who breathes life into earth's people, makes them alive with his own life: 'I am God. I have called you to live right and well. I have taken responsibility for you, kept you safe. I have set you among my people to bind them to me, and provided you as a lighthouse to the nations, To make a start at bringing people into the open, into light: opening blind eyes, releasing prisoners from dungeons, emptying the dark prisons. I am God. That's my name. I don't franchise my glory, don't endorse the no-god idols…'"

True glory is not transferable. It is assigned and ascribed to the God that gives us breath and life. To offer His praise to statues or falsehoods is the evidence of ignorance, mixture, or both. Worshippers are to keep God's name holy.

Chapter Four

THE ALTAR AND THE OFFERING

While ministering in the presence of God, I have said on many occasions, "Worship is our response to the God we see." While this utterance was given by way of inspiration of the Holy Spirit, it is also biblical and evident throughout scripture. We have established this pattern earlier in this book, that God first reveals Himself before requiring worship. What God reveals to us about Him provokes a response out of our hearts that may be categorized as worship.

Worship is our heart's expression and appreciation lifted toward God that reveals Himself in goodness and nearness. Like prayer, worship is a form of communication to God that pleases Him and provokes His response. Worship performs on behalf of the Word of God sent to prosper us in accordance with His perfect will. Worship exemplifies trust, hope, and dependency on God for which we are rewarded. Without faith, it is impossible to please God. Therefore, with faith, we communicate what is pleasurable to heaven and receive a heavenly reward.

In the Old Testament, the place of transaction where God would meet with, perform for, or be remembered by man for His performance was the place where the offering was raised. Offerings were presented to God on an altar, also defined as "a place of slaughter."

The fall of Adam resulted in a breach of fellowship intended to remain eternal and intimate in nature. Until the fall, no sacrifice was required to restore man's relationship with God, for man was created for relationship without wages. There was nothing required of Adam to maintain right standing with God except obedience to His word.

Romans 6:23 (NKJV) —

> "For the wages of sin is death, but the gift of God is eternal life in Christ Jesus our Lord."

When sin entered in so did our debt. For fellowship to be restored between God and man, an exchange had to take place where the life of the innocent covered the life of the guilty. Sacrificial offerings became the method of redemption, restoring right relationship with God. This is why we, the believers, rejoice greatly over the sacrifice of Jesus Christ. He made the former practices of animal sacrifice obsolete.

Leviticus 17:11 (NKJV) —

> "For the life of the flesh is in the blood, and I have given it to you upon the altar to make atonement for your souls; for it is the blood that makes atonement for the soul."

Blood carried a redemptive quality and was a life source. Therefore, it was qualified to be used as an atoning tool for sinful man to regain lost fellowship with God. Unlike those of pagan practice, God's way required that the blood cover the sinner, yet He vehemently opposed the sinner consuming the blood.

Deuteronomy 12:23 (NKJV) —

> "Only be sure that you do not eat the blood, for the blood is the life…"

Pagan cultures believed that if they drank the blood of any particular animal (or person) that they would gain the character or strength of the one whose blood they consumed. God taught Israel to worship to avoid falling prey to denigrating practices such as this as well as to set apart that this God was unlike any other god worshipped in this day.

As long as the sacrificial offering was acceptable, meaning it was ceremonially clean and among the options given in the Book of the Law* God would consume the sacrifice and the offerer was restored. The offering bridged the gap between God and man and became the meeting place of encounter.

Worship in and of itself is an offering. The subject of the altar and the idea of worship are almost synonymous. In essence, they are interchangeable references expressing submission and thanksgiving to God. Both the altar and worship are places of exchange between God and man.

Where an altar is erected, worship takes place.

Where worship takes place today is vastly different than in the days of old. You will see on many occasions how the followers of Christ in the OT would build an altar to remember God's provision and miraculous power along their journeys. At every stop and along the way, they would build an altar naming each to memorialize where victory was experienced, suggesting that the place of worship is transient.

There is no single place of worship. As you walk with God, your journey will include much of your own altar-building. Jesus rebuked the Samaritan woman in John 4 by telling her that a time is coming where the location of worship as in a geological location would become irrelevant. Worship, in truth, is not limited to a geographical location; rather, its source is the heart of a believer who will carry worship with them wherever they go. Jesus taught that what was more significant than the location was that the worship was authentic and offered to the proper authority. We will discuss that in greater detail. For now, let's continue.

The act or the idea of worship in its fullness did not begin with Abraham; rather, it continued with him. Abraham followed patterns of worship practiced by others following the Lord before the day his name was called.

What we see from its first mention in scripture is an outline of what worship is and how the worshipper responds to God. This outline will help us to identify acts of worship throughout scripture.

When we look into all that worship consists of, we see several components that render it complete: an offerer, an offering, a death, a fire, and the offering's recipient

To make worship complete, there must be:

1. An offerer: a person presenting an offering.

2. An offering: the actual thing being presented.

3. A death: living sacrifices were offered after slaying them. No living sacrifice was offered alive. (There were other types of offerings that were not living creatures.)

4. A fire: a consuming force symbolic of the acceptance of the sacrifice.

5. A recipient: In the case of the believer, this is God.

Genesis 6:12-19 (NJKV) —

> *"And God looked upon the earth, and, behold, it was corrupt; for all flesh had corrupted his way upon the earth. And God said unto Noah, The end of all flesh is come before me; for the earth is filled with violence*

through them; and, behold, I will destroy them with the earth. But with thee will I establish my covenant; and thou shalt come into the ark, thou, and thy sons, and thy wife, and thy sons' wives with thee. And of every living thing of all flesh, two of every sort shalt thou bring into the ark, to keep them alive with thee; they shall be male and female."

God decided to establish a covenant with Noah after preserving his life on the ark that he was instructed to build. He created man for relationship, yet man's continual choices to follow after darkness influenced generations to walk further away from Him. His indignation gave way to destruction, but even in the destruction, mercy was at its core. He preserved an upright man, his family, and the couples of two of every other living creature made in the beginning. God's intention to destroy all living things was not born of evil, for there is no evil in God.

Genesis 6:6 (NKJV) —

"And the Lord was sorry that He had made man on the earth and He was grieved in His heart."

The Lord was not sorry in the sense of having made a mistake. Making man was never considered a mistake. God is perfect in all of His ways always. It is man's flaws that determine the courses of life that lead to darkness and all that darkness invites. What brought God's heart sorrow was that who man became was an inaccurate reflection of His original intention. The destruction He authorized offered a cleansing of the earth, a restart for all mankind. This made way for the earth's revival and restoration that was ushered in by Noah's worship.

Despite the Lord's disappointment in man's accelerated corruption in Noah, God found grace.

Let's take a closer look at the power of Noah's worship seen in this account. Before we take a look, allow me to erect an altar right here as I am compelled to give God thanks for the opportunity to become a change agent in your life.

> *"Father, I thank You for breakthrough. Father, I lift up this moment to You. I memorialize this entire book-writing journey with You. I thank You, Lord, for making me Your scribe, for anointing my fingers to write, and for giving me the ability to communicate Your heart in soundness to Your people. Lord, I appreciate You choosing me, and I give You my yes all over again, even at this moment. If I were to erect a physical altar before You and give it a name, I would call this altar 'Thank You For Using Me.' Thank You for calling me; thank You for making me Your own; thank You for making me Your vessel; thank You for making me Your microphone; thank You for making me Your scribe; thank You for making me an example for You. Father, thank You for making me a light to shine and for calling and commissioning me to such an impactful work for the kingdom. Thank You, Father. Thank You."*

When the floods receded, Noah built an altar to God. Before Noah celebrated his release with his family or stretched his legs on dry ground, he first worshipped the Lord. This single act of worship gained God's attention in such a way that it should never be forgotten.

Genesis 8:15-20 (NKJV) —

> *"Then God spoke to Noah, saying, 'Go out of the ark, you and your wife, and your sons and your sons' wives with you. Bring out with you every living thing of all flesh that is with you: birds and cattle and every creeping thing that creeps on the earth, so that they may abound on the earth, and be fruitful and multiply on the earth.' So Noah went out, and his sons and his wife and his sons' wives with him. Every animal, every creeping thing, every bird, and whatever creeps on the earth, according to their families, went out of the ark. Then Noah built an altar to the Lord, and took of every clean animal and every clean bird, and offered burnt offerings on the altar."*

God releases Noah from the ark with everything He commanded him to preserve. The wisdom of God in Noah's preservation was this: the male and female species whose lives were maintained along with Noah and his family would suffice to replenish the earth with the life God destroyed. God had restoration on His mind, and Noah had worship on his heart. God's mind and Noah's heart collided and what came forth was God's perfect plan that we are still living under today. Re-read verse 20 —

> *"Then Noah built an altar to the Lord, and took of every **clean** animal and every clean bird, and offered burnt offerings on the altar."*

Clean animals were deemed ceremonially pure and acceptable offerings set forth in the Levitical Law (Leviticus 11:1-8). Not only did Noah offer every clean animal as in that which was acceptable to God, but the clean sacrifices were also male in species. This means that Noah immediately offered the animals possessing the seed required to reproduce. How would the remnant of animals reproduce now that Noah offered the males to God? What Noah did was so powerful! He offered his potential for increase, something that wasn't even required of him at that moment.

God did not ask Noah for worship here. Unlike Abraham, Noah did not respond to God's instruction in requesting a sacrifice. Instead, Noah responded to his own heart of gratitude. He and his family were saved from what destroyed every other family. God, in His mercy, had given Noah an exclusive experience that would mark the remainder of his life and many generations to follow. Without instruction, Noah built an altar. As a result, God was pleased.

Genesis 8:20-21 (KJV) —

> *"And the Lord smelled a soothing aroma. Then the Lord said in His heart, 'I will never again curse the ground for man's sake, although the imagination of man's heart is evil from his youth; nor will I again destroy every living thing as I have done.' While the earth remains,*

seedtime and harvest, cold and heat, winter and summer, and day and night shall not cease."

What this covenant did was reestablish the Father's original intention and all He created for the benefit of man from the beginning. "Seedtime and harvest, cold and heat, winter and summer, day and night" was not a new concept to God. Those cycles were already established when He set forth creation day by day in Genesis chapter one. God's original intention was interrupted by man's corruption which led to the destruction that could have deterred destiny for all mankind had not this man worshiped the way that he did. Worship provokes and perpetuates the original intention of God in our lives. This is the power of worship as seen in scripture.

So, all the male species of all the clean animals were offered to God which means they were slain first yet somehow God replenished the earth with what was offered. Herein lies God's supernatural provision given to the worshipper in response to what is offered on the altar. This is also why, for many years, I have learned that tithing is an act of worship. What Noah did when he built that altar was communicate total dependency and trust in God. God loves when we trust Him. He promises that those that trust in Him would never be put to shame.

Noah's offering took the power to produce out of his hands and put it in the hands of God instead. This form of worship is honorable and has been met with supernatural abundance even until today.

This is the premise of the tithe offering. It was not until thousands of years later that the word of the Lord came to Malachi regarding the tithe. Yet twice in Genesis, we see our patriarchs in the faith offering up a tenth of their provision to God in response to God's preservation. Abraham tithed to Melchizedek who was a type of Christ and Jacob vowed to give God a tenth of all. They offered up a tenth, and it was accounted as righteousness. How much more does God respond to the man that gives Him their all?

The day I fell in love with God, I fell in love with God. My surrender to Him was not monolithic. I did not just give the Lord my Sunday mornings and an afternoon on Wednesdays. When I received salvation, I gave Him all of me. In some kind of way, I understood that not only did God want me, but He wanted all of me. I did not fight the surrender. In times of encounter, I came to know Him and trust Him entirely. This made surrender easy. Before receiving salvation which I received during my tenure in federal prison, I had no idea what I would do when I got behind the prison gates. I contemplated how many fights I may have if someone were to attempt to steal my food. I contemplated becoming someone's girlfriend, whether an inmate or a guard. Life had begun to make me bitter, and with a hardened heart now open to new vices, I can honestly say I don't know what I would have done had God not snatched me out of the pit I was in by preserving me with that prison sentence. I did not know what I planned to do but I did know I did not anticipate an encounter with Jesus.

I gave Him my full surrender, and in exchange for my life, God gave me His. It was more than the salvation I received on that sunny Sunday. On that day, I received abundance. I began to dream bigger in God after salvation than I had ever dreamed. And when my life was restored after my release, my accelerated success in the beauty industry was the fruit of my faith regarding money. I would anticipate Sunday's tithing opportunity, week by week, and calculate my earnings to a T to ensure I was not short-changing God. But there were several times when I was provoked to give it all, and I did so without hesitation. Somewhere in my spirit, I knew that the God that supplied the seed would meet every pending need with His supernatural power. Over and over, He did just that. I gave Him my appetite for food, my appetite for sex, and my appetite for attention. He consumed it all on the altar of my heart and gave me what I will never have to give up again. He gave me Him. God's response to those areas of worship filled my life in such a way that it is undeniable. I did not anticipate the change that would come when I offered my all. I just knew I could trust God with every part of me, and for me, that was enough. I did not intend to exchange anything at the time. My only intention was to surrender. My way did not fulfill me. I offered myself to people that turned their backs on me. I offered myself to men that didn't always honor me. Now, I would become God's offering and see what He would do with what man did not seem to accept or honor consistently.

The worshipper responds to God's preservation with an offering of thanksgiving, trust, and dependency. God, the receiver of worship, responds to man's offering by reaffirming the covenant.

In Greek, the altar is defined as "the place of slaughter." With Christ as our living example, the altar of this dispensation of grace relies on your surrender to be made effective. Precious in the sight of the Lord is the death of His saints. It is not our physical death that brings God delight. It is our surrender, our yielding, our obedience, and our trust that converts our lives to a liquid form that we may remain poured out before Him, uninhibited in any way. The altar is where the worshipper lives, and the worshipper lives on the altar. The altar is now wherever you lift your heart to give honor to a God that kept you in every way He has kept you.

You are the offering He now requires. It is no longer any clean animal or bird. Now that Christ has become our atonement once and for all, the offering is you and the altar is your heart.

Chapter Five

UNPURIFIED FORMS OF WORSHIP

The same Holy Spirit who revealed Christ's lordship also teaches you to denounce all idols and leads you into truth. I'm baffled that so many believers reject wisdom concerning idolatry. The same Bible used to command blessings into our lives also curses works of darkness that too many believers follow. The fact is that men love darkness rather than light, yet in His mercy, He extends grace for our ignorance. The grace He extends gives us room and time to be disciples, but it does not automatically shut the doors we open when we choose to delve into idolatry.

Our salvation and induction into the kingdom require our belief and confession. In this, we can pull the principle that belief grants us access to portals or openings into unseen realms. It is the hope of the Father and ministry leaders that we only enter into heavenly portals that are purified and made available to us by God. The unfortunate reality is that the god of this world offers portals also; however, his portals lead to death, if not natural then most certainly spiritual. He is a liar and a deceiver, and the enemy has no shame. He will disguise himself with light to deceive those in search of enlightenment.

2 Corinthians 11:14-15 (MSG) —

"And no wonder! Satan does it all the time, dressing up as a beautiful angel of light. So, it shouldn't surprise us when his servants masquerade as servants of God. But they're not getting by with anything. They'll pay for it in the end. Look at what he did in the Garden with Eve"

Genesis 3:9-13 (NKJV) —

Deception can look so pure and peaceful to the undiscerning.

"The Lord God called to Adam and said to him, 'Where are you?' So he said, 'I heard your voice in the garden, and I was afraid because I was naked and I hid myself.' And He said, 'Who told you that you were naked? Have you eaten from the tree of which I commanded you that you should not eat?' Then the man said, 'The woman whom you gave to be with me, she gave me of the tree, and I ate.'"

Following the enemy's way led to Adam's shame, fear, and distance from God. He is a mocker of God's people. The enemy is not your friend. All he can offer is a lie for there is no truth in him at all. He wants to dissuade as many people as possible from trusting and following God because although the enemy is evil, he likes company. He does not want to endure destruction alone. He cannot cross back over where you are (or where you want to be) into the kingdom of light. His trajectory is set, and his eternity awaits him. He wants you to be where he is headed. If he cannot get you there, he will deceive you into a weakness that looks like wit, intelligence, awareness, openness, and peace. It is important that you read this account in its fullness to follow along.

Genesis 3:1-7 (AMP) —

"Now the serpent was more crafty (subtle, skilled in deceit) than any living creature of the field which the Lord God had made. And the serpent (Satan) said to the woman, 'Can it really be that God has said, 'You shall not eat from any tree of the garden?' And the woman said

to the serpent, 'We may eat fruit from the trees of the garden, except the fruit from the tree which is in the middle of the garden. God said, 'You shall not eat from it nor touch it, otherwise you will die.' But the serpent said to the woman, 'You certainly will not die! For God knows that on the day you eat from it your eyes will be opened [that is, you will have greater awareness], and you will be like God, knowing [the difference between] good and evil.' And when the woman saw that the tree was good for food and that it was delightful to look at, and a tree to be desired in order to make one wise and insightful, she took some of its fruit and ate it; and she also gave some to her husband with her, and he ate. Then the eyes of the two of them were opened [that is, their awareness increased], and they knew that they were naked, and they fastened fig leaves together and made themselves coverings."

Eve accessed the wrong portal when she obeyed the deceiver. Portals of darkness became available when Eve allowed deception to win. When God called to them in the garden, you must understand that God was not standing by a palm tree while Adam and Eve stood nearby the orange groves. God is now and was at that time in heaven in the uppermost chamber. God communicates to us through a portal which is an unseen opening. This is the same way He communicates with us today—through the vehicle of prayer.

The serpent became the conduit of demonic influence intended to keep Eve and Adam from God's fullness by opening them up to a realm of intrigue leading to their separation.

Genesis 2:15-17 (AMP) —

"So the Lord God took the man [He had made] and settled him in the Garden of Eden to cultivate and keep it. And the Lord God commanded the man, saying, 'You may freely (unconditionally) eat [the fruit] from every tree of the garden; but [only] from the tree of knowledge of good

and evil you shall not eat, otherwise, on the day that you eat from it, you shall most certainly die [because of your disobedience]."

God was protecting the gaze of His first son and daughter by disallowing them access to that realm. His instructions were given to fortify their focus, fueling uninterrupted fellowship with their Father. Although the serpent had access to the garden, his proximity to its residents would have no footing if left ignored. Eve could have disregarded him while ignoring the conversation. Ignoring darkness, as in disregarding it as wisdom, is not ignorant. In fact, it is wise.

Do not be deceived by the enemy's device of universal acceptance. Resist the enemy and he will flee is what the Bible says in James 4:7. To effectively resist the enemy, the enemy must first be recognized. It was not his form that revealed the serpent as a tool of Satan; it was his words revealing that his wisdom was from another source of a much lower degree.

Resisting happens when we have the light of God to behold and remain fixed on purpose. When we yield to darkness, it is because we are no longer beholding God's light. When we yield, it is because we have given our attention to what is from another realm. For how could man see God's light and choose His enemy's way instead?

In His admonition to refrain from the tree of the knowledge of good and evil, the Lord was protecting their focus from realms that would disrupt their fellowship. Although it was not called worship at that time, the lifestyle Adam and Eve lived prior to the fall was indeed a lifestyle of worship. If we knew what deception creates in us and around us, we would flee and never return. Before the fall, discernment wasn't necessary. Continual fellowship with the light would have dispelled darkness before it manifested. Before the fall, their gaze was fixed. Life in Eden reflected the beauty of perfect fellowship. Their introduction to the dark realm by way of their disobedience presented them with an option of whom they should serve.

Should they obey the One that gave them life or the one that fed them lies? They were naked all along but didn't know it until this portal opened. They no longer saw their spiritual stature; they now saw their nature. They paid attention to themselves, their acts, their sin, and their shame. As such, they went into hiding, no longer seeing or seeking their God.

That is the root of religion. It is man-focused and demonic from its root. Self-awareness and self-ridden shame turn us away from God even while His presence is available. Deceit is often successful because ingrained in its form is a level of truth. The serpent used some of what God said intermingled with demonic order. What he suggested only sounded slightly off. This is what makes it so easy to fall prey to impure forms of worship and obedience. It isn't that deception is 100% false; it's the mixture of the pure that renders it false and unacceptable to the believer.

Satan's pattern of altar building is a copy of what he experienced in Heaven. He was so close to God and familiar with the atmospheres of glory that he repackaged it; he rebranded satanic glory and presents it as light. His agenda is openness, universal acceptance, while the Word of God says the way is narrow (Matthew 7:14). The enemy perverts the Word and plans of God for believers by suggesting that it is restrictive and that somehow, God who authored your salvation and has come to give you abundance wants to limit your freedom. The devil is a liar. He deceived Eve by dismantling her belief system with mere suggestions. His manner of movement is manipulation and provocation, and his entry points include the following:

The lust of the eye

The lust of the flesh

The pride of life.

To deny deception the success it's after, you must overcome those three areas like Jesus did. That is how Christ overcame Satan's attempt to steal worship from Him after His 40 days of fasting. That is also how you know that worship is highly valued in the unseen worlds of light and darkness. Satan, the author of audacity, approached Christ and asked Him for worship. As stated earlier, Satan didn't parade demons before Jesus, which would have been too obvious a solicitation. Satan tempted Jesus with worship by presenting Him with opportunity. This is where the believer must grow in discernment and apply wisdom.

Luke 4:5-10 (NKJV) —

> *"And the devil, taking him up into a high mountain, shewed unto him all the kingdoms of the world in a moment of time. And the devil said unto him, All this power will I give thee, and the glory of them: for that is delivered unto me; and to whomsoever I will I give it. If thou therefore wilt worship me, all shall be thine. And Jesus answered and said unto him, Get thee behind me, Satan: for it is written, Thou shalt worship the Lord thy God, and him only shalt thou serve. And he brought him to Jerusalem, and set him on a pinnacle of the temple, and said unto him, If thou be the Son of God, cast thyself down from hence: For it is written, He shall give his angels charge over thee, to keep thee: And in their hands they shall bear thee up, lest at any time thou dash thy foot against a stone. And Jesus answering said unto him, It is said, Thou shalt not tempt the Lord thy God."*

This fallen angel, evicted from heaven and remanded to earth for a set time until his eternal fate, goes around asking for worship, just not as boldly as he did in this account with Jesus. Any way the enemy can successfully present darkness, he will do it. Some, like Satanists and blatant workers of the dark realm, openly and actively seek darkness; they are aware of their intention. Others who understand that Satan is a foe of the kingdom, he grabs in more subtle ways. His campaign does not present witches on posters or T-shirts.

No, his campaign looks like light, peace, and universal acceptance.

Before I came into the faith, there was a woman I knew who was a strong woman of God and a mighty woman of prayer. Cultural affinity had her, at times, exposed to forms of worship that were unholy according to biblical standards. She introduced me to a woman from Panama who practiced what I would come to know as Santería, a form of white witchcraft often perpetrated by Christians from the Caribbean diaspora.

I loved that woman. She was so cool and so much fun and nothing about anything she did seemed dark. One day, she invited me to a prayer meeting that she had with some of her friends. During this prayer meeting, they had a beautiful table set up with a white tablecloth. It was a sacramental feast, and I still remember the candles burning. I sensed something in the room that I couldn't identify, but it wasn't necessarily scary. Each of the women began to pray. One began to blow into a cigar. She inhaled the smoke from the wide end of the cigar and blew it out of the smaller end because they believed that the smoke would come out in the form of whatever spirit was present in the room. They went around the table and prayed before approaching me and asking me to pray. I didn't want to pray because I honestly didn't know how to pray at that time. They put a white sheet around me, swaddling me. They began to pray, and they said that there was a white light shining around me. I remember crying and rocking but I can't readily recall what I said. They told me that I was marked for special things or something of that nature. They said I reminded them of Mary, the mother of Jesus, and that I was marked for prayer.

I never forgot that night, but I didn't actually know what happened. What I later came to understand was that Santería was a type of Obeah, a kind of sorcery. Those ladies genuinely loved me, but the impure worship they introduced me to opened doors to devils in my life that I would have to later close through deliverance.

Another time, this woman came to my house to conduct a spiritual cleansing. I had heard of spiritual cleansings and was fascinated by the concept.

When she came to my house for the cleansing, she had a bottle of clear liquor and a cigar. She walked through my house, and she spoke in a language I did not understand. She lit a candle, and she did the same thing with the cigar that I remember her doing that night in prayer. Again, she inhaled from the wide end and blew out from the small end. The smoke would take the form of whatever spirit was in the house, and that's how she identified what she needed to cleanse.

She identified the form of an extremely dark, handsome man with beautiful white teeth, and she called his name—Wayne. What she did not know was that my first adult love, murdered on February 4, 1999, was named Wayne. He was the most handsome, dark-chocolate man I had ever seen, and although he was a cheater, he loved some Ngina. I had never loved a man with such intensity, so much so that the desperation and depression that followed his murder ultimately led to the crime I committed that led me to prison. His spirit was in my house. By that time, it had to have been a year or two since his murder, but my heart held on to the man I loved. She saw his spirit in my house, and yet I called that cleansing.

Here is the revelation: How could I consider her cleansing effective if she pulled up the image of a man in a place he had never lived? What she discovered was the presence of a man that died in another country. Yet, while I was living in a completely different place, his spirit appeared! It would become clear to me that instead of "cleansing" (removing, getting rid of, eliminating, etc.), what was actually taking place was quite the opposite. What I thought was a cleansing was actually an invitation. Doors were being opened that became an invitation to death.

For at least a year prior to his death, I had the same dream of his funeral. In the dream, I was standing at his funeral wearing a black dress and pink lipstick with my hair in curls. Behind me was a red BMW and beautiful greenery. There were no other details to my dream other than what I just described. I had this dream a minimum of 12 times.

After his death was announced, his family called me. I flew to Jamaica to attend the funeral. We took some pictures, and I went home. I don't recall how much time transpired between the day his body was laid to rest and the time I went through my stacks of photos, but I later went through my pictures and realized that the exact image in my dream was captured in the photos I took. From the greenery and red BMW to the lipstick and the curls, everything was the exact same. I always knew I was a dreamer and that there were spiritual implications to my dreams, but I didn't attribute the spiritual realities to the God I now know. My dreams would manifest very quickly which frightened me when I began to dream of my own funeral.

Yes!

I began to dream of my own funeral. At my funeral, it was as if I was dreaming to see who came and what they had to say about the person in the casket. It scared me because if I knew anything, I knew that my dreams come true. Was I going to die like Wayne?

When I got to prison, the very first prophetic word I ever received was this: "You better be lucky that the Lord brought you behind these prison walls because the enemy was going to kill you." What I eventually discovered through discipleship in the Word was that the opening of demonic doors leads to destruction and death. In my case, death was literal. The enemy was after my life, and I had no way to shut those doors except by the delivering power of God. I had done so many things I thought to be innocent, yet my ignorance offered no mercy. Fear, torment, oppression, depression, and confusion are just a few of the darts that hell launched at me. I went to psychics because I thought it was okay. I played with Ouija boards and watched scary movies, and to this day, I can't be around woods as God is still delivering me from the fears that entrapped my soul. In our ignorance, we open doors all of the time. Once we enter, we cannot dictate the enemy's plan for us there. We become open game for the enemy to wreak havoc in our lives, not designed to strengthen us but to destroy us.

As believers, we should never find ourselves partaking in such practices as necromancy (communicating with the dead), consulting psychics, witches, mediums, and workers of witchcraft, using or believing in the help of spirit guides, tarot cards, or fraternizing with familiar spirits, indulging in yoga, crystal readings, or cleansings, etc. Those are ungodly practices that aid in creating a barrier between us and our Father. The root of each of these practices mentioned is paganism and false worship and none of it is a consecrated form of worship. Consulting darkness and expecting light to be revealed is unbiblical and non-sensical.

In 1 Samuel 28:3-25, King Saul lamented over the death of the prophet Samuel and sought a familiar spirit, or witch, for guidance. For this, he was sharply rebuked. He had become accustomed to the leading voice of the prophet and because of his rebellion, greed, and disobedience, he lost his seat of authority and began to question his safety in battle. The prophet Samuel had died, and God sent him no further instruction. In his desperation, he sought the work that only a witch could perform, believing it would produce a God-authored result. He needed help and confirmation for the battle ahead of him and his prophet was now dead. So, he found a witch to bring up the spirit of Prophet Samuel to help him decide whether to go to war. His pursuit of a spirit guide from darkness was provoked by desperation, not faith. Even the witch herself questioned Saul's motive, believing that he was of God.

Communicating with the dead on any level, by any believer, is forbidden because not only does it create a false sense of peace, but it also opens doors to darkness. It activates portals of darkness that will send you something you may not expect.

Deuteronomy 18: 9-14 (AMP) —

"When you enter the land which the Lord your God is giving you, you shall not learn to imitate the detestable (repulsive) practices of those nations. There shall not be found among you anyone who makes his son or daughter pass through the fire [as a sacrifice], one who uses divination and fortune-telling, one who practices witchcraft, or one who interprets omens, or a sorcerer, or one who casts a charm or spell, or a medium, or a spiritist, or a necromancer [who seeks the dead]. For everyone who does these things is utterly repulsive to the Lord, and because of these detestable practices the Lord your God is driving them out before you. You shall be blameless (complete, perfect) before the Lord your God. For these nations which you shall dispossess listen to those who practice witchcraft and to diviners and fortune-tellers, but as for you, the Lord your God has not allowed you to do so."

Likewise, the overemphasis on information extracted from the study of the stars, (i.e., astrology and numerology) and other forms of false worship also reveal deceit and disbelief. The Wise Men followed the star that was prophesied in the book of Daniel to reveal Christ's birth. Rightly dividing the prophecy, they followed the star to determine the location of the Messiah sent to the earth. What they did not do was worship the star that led them there. This is where many fall into error. Who worships the created thing above the Creator? Who puts faith in a created thing above the Creator?

Moses was anguished to hear that just moments after leaving the children of Israel, who were led out of captivity and experienced miraculous provision by God, made themselves an object of worship. They removed their earrings, melted them in fire, and shaped the gold into a calf. They were so utterly desperate to worship that they created their own god. They worshipped an object that was made by their own hands. Worshippers of Christ bow, yield, and look to no other God. It is the One, true living God that supplies all our needs according to His riches in glory. This supply cannot be sourced from a god of your choice or your making. You will find your supply in purity in God.

Isaiah 47:12-15 (NKJV) —

> *"You are wearied in the multitude of your counsels;*
> *Let now the astrologers, the stargazers,*
> *And the monthly prognosticators*
> *Stand up and save you*
> *From what shall come upon you.*
> *Behold, they shall be as stubble,*
> *The fire shall burn them;*
> *They shall not deliver themselves*
> *From the power of the flame;*
> *It shall not be a coal to be warmed by,*
> *Nor a fire to sit before!*
> *Thus shall they be to you*
> *With whom you have labored,*
> *Your merchants from your youth;*
> *They shall wander each one to his quarter.*
> *No one shall save you."*

According to Hebrews 1:3, all things created are sustained by the glory of His power. That said, while God is manifested in His creation, His creation does not usurp His seat on the throne and therefore cannot warrant your worship. God created crystals but they are subject to Him; they don't replace Him. You don't look to crystals for guidance and answers; you look to Who created them.

The same God that requires our exclusive worship condemns these practices, yet so many believers find it okay. If this is you, the compromise you have been living in comes to an end today. The strength of your walk with

God is weakened by your trust in the created thing and not the Creator. Let's look to Joshua 7:20-25, and I really want you to read this —

"And Achan answered Joshua and said, 'Indeed I have sinned against the Lord God of Israel, and this is what I have done: When I saw among the spoils a beautiful Babylonian garment, two hundred shekels of silver, and a wedge of gold weighing fifty shekels, I coveted them and took them. And there they are, hidden in the earth in the midst of my tent, with the silver under it.' So Joshua sent messengers, and they ran to the ten; and there it was, hidden in his tent, with the silver under. And they took them from the midst of the tent, brought them to Joshua and to all the children of Israel, and laid them out before the Lord. Then Joshua, and all Israel with him, took Achan the son of Zerah, the silver, the garment, the wedge of gold, his sons, his daughters, his oxen, his donkeys, his sheep, his tent, and all that he had, and they brought them to the Valley of Achor. And Joshua said, 'Why have you troubled us? The Lord will trouble you this day.' So all Israel stoned him with stones; and they burned them with fire after they had stoned them with stones."

The accursed thing held onto by Achan in Joshua 6:18 was not tarot cards. The accursed thing was the thing God told him not to touch. What made it accursed was that it was against God's instruction. Many believe that because crystals are natural materials and sage is an herb made by God, even used in scripture, applying it to your life for peace makes it acceptable. How many other people pervert the use of a thing and call it good? Pedophiliacs pervert the accessibility to young children and call it good. Drug addicts pervert access to cannabis and call it good. What makes you think that the misuse of a thing guided by your unbelief and mistrust will somehow make it good? The destruction that comes to us by way of doors we open through the worship of idols in any form does not look like being burned with fire in front of your peers. What it creates is a form of death manifesting in a form of separation from the God you say you trust.

Likewise, the gift that psychics and tarot card readers operate in that gain your attention is a perverted form of the prophetic. Seeing into realms of the spirit is a God-ordained gift available to all. While some are called to the office of the prophet, or others called "seers" by way of divine design, the unsubjected gift to see and tap into spiritual realms must be accessed by the authority given by God. Otherwise, the application of the gift is unauthorized, unholy, and cannot be trusted. Always keep in mind that the author of confusion leading many into darkness is extremely familiar with the unseen world. By satanic power, information is disseminated in part to gain your attention and trust to draw you into a false sense of hope.

What is he after?

First, your attention. Then, your trust.

His mode of operation will always include perversion, as in an exchange of truth for mixture.

For many people, it is cultural conformity and affinity that leads to these practices that too many deem acceptable. So what it was the practice of the Indigenous people of the land. The Creator of all things was available even when some chose to follow other gods. Moreover, He was available for worship long before idols were established. Thus, it is entirely false to believe that pagan worship was first. Those who ascribe to such practices are holding onto the cultural practices of people who had their beginning elsewhere.

In Ur of the Chaldeans, the place from which Abraham was called, many gods were worshipped. A few of their names were Marduk, Sin, Inanna, Utu, Bel, Baal, Ashur, and others. Among those forms of worship were the practices of incense burning, energy readings, the worship of statues, the practice of yoga, chanting, levitations, meditations, human sacrificing, drinking blood, the misuse of herbal practices, and so much more.

There was a god of fertility, a god of the harvest, a god of the sun, moon, and stars, a god of the animal kingdom, and the list goes on.

Idol worship is still practiced today, all of which is rooted in the lie that there are many ways of acceptable worship to God. Abraham followed the God of Heaven; he worshipped idols, too. God created crystals, but they are subject to Him; they don't replace Him.

Idol worship is more about your trust than your choice. Because of Jesus' sacrifice, we are now the offering. Worship of idols is not your choice; it's about your trust, and what I mean by that is this: When and if you really trust God, you will believe that He would do for you what you desire those other idolatrous things to do for you. See, people choose to burn sage because they believe it brings peace by driving out darkness and demons. I have witnessed demonic manifestations on many occasions and not one time did deliverance take place because sage was in the room. Demons flee in the name of Jesus.

1 John 3:8 (NKJV) —

"For this purpose the Son of God was manifested, that He might destroy the works of the devil."

What drives our darkness is the light of Christ. No herb shares His glory.

If you believe that peace comes from an herb, it's because you really don't believe peace comes from God. You can go to the spa, intending to enjoy a self-care day, understanding that relaxation methods soothe the soul. You can listen to soft jazz or instrumental spa sounds to calm your mind, understanding that setting an atmosphere of peace can be conducive to your peace of mind. However, you cannot ascribe kingdom power to any of it, replacing the use of the word for created matter.

What you believe determines what you worship and how you worship. What you believe is paramount to your foundation of worship. Where there are gaps in your foundation caused by stony ground, cultural pride, open doors, false teachings, etc. an enemy of deception will enter in tumbling blocks and show up in your worship.

The word "yoga" means "to join, to yoke or unite." Its origin is found in ancient India, and it entails the practice of uniting individual consciousness with divine consciousness through meditation and posing stretches It is demonically branded as a form of "spiritual development" said to train the body and mind to become more aware of itself and combat the forces of life that come to interrupt the body's peace or harmony. Your mind should be renewed by the word of God, not the impure practice of yoga.

It is branded with the supposed benefits it brings to the body but keeps hidden the dark doors that are opened. Who you become united with in the practice and positioning yoga teaches is a false god. Just stretch. Meditate on the word of God. Do Pilates to strengthen the core and elongate the body. By engaging in yoga poses you are assuming positions of worship and become the offering to the 330 million Hindu gods. The Lord your God is one. Your peace is in Him. The harmony you look to attain in the practice of yoga, your body is supernaturally designed to balance safer ways.

Crystal readings or readings of other kinds, such as that of tarot cards or psychics, are said to bring clarity to your reality and/or help with the release of emotional blockages for balance's sake. The Bible tells us to examine ourselves.

2 Corinthians 13:5 (NKJV) —

"Examine yourselves as to whether you are in the faith. Test yourselves. Do you not know yourselves, that Jesus Christ is in you?"

You have a greater ability than any crystal to confess the contents of your heart to God for purification. For the believer, our insight is Divine and Holy, and His name is Jesus the Christ who reveals all things to us by the Holy Spirit. A crystal cannot convey what Holy Spirit can and should not be any believer's source of enlightenment. You depend on crystals and psychic readings, but have you ever submitted yourself to a tried and tested prophetic voice? A spirit of divination, the spirit sharing information through such vices, is not holy and cannot guide you into a destiny created by God. Seek truth by the Spirit of Truth. Grace and truth come through Jesus Christ.

John 1:17 (NKJV) —

"For the law was given through Moses, but grace and truth came through Jesus Christ."

Followers of truth, listen to me: There is no mixture in truth. Once you begin to add mixture to truth, its power is dissolved, and darkness is invited in. Imagine a glass of water and telling yourself that it's okay to add just a pinch of Kool-Aid. What you've now added to the water changes its color, content, and condition. Once you add any substance other than that which is water, you have tainted it entirely. Water only remains water if water is added. Even one drop of anything otherwise alters its content. Followers of truth are not to mix truth with falsehoods of any kind.

Remain pure in worship and repent of any such practices. Seek the Light, for light so that your light is not darkness in disguise.

Chapter Six

THE ACCEPTABLE OFFERING IS YOU — YOU ARE WORTHY TO WORSHIP

The greatest enemy to our pursuit of God is self-perception. This is why renewing our minds by living, applying, and praying the Word of God are essential. No level of relationship from parent to spouse or child mirrors the love of God in fullness. While we cannot deny the beauty of parental, sibling, or romantic love, it remains substandard, at best, to the agape love of God. No one loves you as perfectly as God. His love is without interruption or interrogation. God's love is not dispensed upon the flawless and withheld from the evil. God's love is not earned, deserved, or provoked. God is love.

1 John 4:8 (AMP) —

> "The one who does not love has not become acquainted with God [does not and never did know Him], for God is love. [He is the originator of love, and it is an enduring attribute of His nature.]"

The Song of Solomon describes love as strong as death. Love is a permanent, irrevocable fixture. Unfortunately, what we cannot say of mankind, we can most assuredly say of God in faith. His love for you is endless and boundless. God's love for you is more expansive than the sky; it is deeper than the ocean and vaster than any continent. God's love for us is more profound and prolific than the best poem you've ever heard or the best book you've ever read. God's love is perfect and deserving of your attention.

Man's love is conditional. As such, the inconsistency we experience from those that say they love us, including our parents and loved ones, can taint our frame of reference regarding true, pure love.

I was abandoned by my father, and from a very young age, I internalized rejection as my norm. In my innocence, I believed that love was what I witnessed and experienced in life. I saw couples, married and unmarried, that "loved each other" (or so I thought), that abused one another, cheated on one another, and at times, disrespected one another. I never questioned that love existed between those I grew up around or was exposed to. I simply believed that my experiences with them defined love as opposed to love being defined on its own. I never fathomed a father not loving their daughter or any mother not loving their son. I just accepted that love sometimes abandons, sometimes hurts, and sometimes lies. I had no idea, until after growing in the knowledge of God's love for me, that what I accepted as true love was actually a counterfeit. What I accepted as real was a perverted version. Now, the love of my mother and some family members was more than enough for me to lean on, but it wasn't only their expression of love that shaped me.

The love I thought was genuine provoked insecurity and fears of all kinds. I remember how rejection discipled me into believing that I must have caused my father to remain absent. I have two siblings, each of whom was impacted by his abandonment, but only I could internalize and interpret its impact on me. I remember pondering these thoughts:

Why wouldn't he want me?

Why did he leave me?

To this very day, saying the word "dad" makes me extremely uncomfortable because aside from my grandfather, I had not experienced the dad side of fatherhood. It caused me to question my worth in ways that led to unvocalized self-esteem issues and insecurities. I was void of the affirmation that comes from a father, and I envied the few friends I had that were daddy's girls. Imperfect love produced a fear deep in my impressionable heart before I had the opportunity to recognize its impurity. It was the discovery of my Father's love that healed that wound.

How?

Because God's love is perfect, and perfect love casts out fear.

1 John 4:18 (NKJV) —

> "There is no fear in love; but perfect love casteth out fear: because fear hath torment. He that feareth is not made perfect in love."

Love that is fixed and full does not leave room for fear of abandonment, rejection, or abusive punishment. We should be mature enough to understand that healthy love can be correct without abuse. Love does not torment, berate, or abuse in any way, shape, or form. Yet, there is a corrective element to love that should be accepted. The Bible teaches us that whom the Lord loves, He chastens.

Proverbs 3:12 (NKJV) —

> "For whom the Lord loves He corrects, just as a father the son in whom he delights."

Man is not perfect outside of the imputed perfection of Christ. Therefore, we cannot expect from man all of the amazing characteristics of God as often as we want. We must discern the difference and govern ourselves accordingly. The cruelty of abuse of any form, whether passive, aggressive, or passive-aggressive is that it can send a person into hiding in shame, guilt, and condemnation. Nothing God exposes to us about us is done to abuse or harm or hurt us. God's correction, or chastisement, is to protect us; always for our good.

In this chapter, we will focus on your worth to God to undo the false impression that anything you could do could turn his love away, rendering you unworthy. Every fault in your body, mind, and soul is not only able to be corrected by the power of the blood of Jesus but it's covered at the sacrifice He became for you. He perfected the most imperfect parts of your being and stained you with His perfection so that you never have to strive for it.

Religion would teach you that because of your faults, God hates you or because of your frailties that God will deny you access, but the power of the cross and the gospel of salvation calls religion a liar. You are worthy to God! If you were the only one alive, Christ's story would remain the same. The Bible declares that angels in heaven rejoice at the salvation of one who crosses over from the kingdom of darkness into the kingdom of light. All of heaven rejoiced the day you said, "Jesus, I believe that You are Lord, and the power of that confession has rendered You clean, holy, and deserving in the eyes of our Father."

If you need to read that again before reading another line of this book, go back and read it again until you believe it because this understanding is required for you to accept the fullness offered to you because of your faith in Christ. In Him, you are son and daughter of irrevocable covenant. Unless you deny His lordship and accomplishment on the cross, undoing what your faith has granted you access to, God offers darkness no refunds. You have been bought with a price by the One who owns it all. No credit or money market account can yield enough interest to pay for what God covered for you.

The beauty and the truth of the gospel are that Jesus Christ your Messiah has made a decision to forgive you for the sin of your past, your present, and your future.

Hebrews 10:16-17 (NKJV) —

> "This is the covenant that I will make with them after those days, saith the Lord, I will put my laws into their hearts, and in their minds will I write them; And their sins and iniquities will I remember no more."

This covenant that remains to this day was born out of mercy that extended from generation to generation. Keep in mind that the DNA that ran through Noah's veins before God destroyed the earth and preserved him in the ark was mingled with blood that produced the evil that made God repent for making man in the first place. God did not destroy the bloodline. He took man of the same nature as the one who was introduced into the world, and He taught him His way by leading him through a life of worship (Romans 3:23). By one man's sin, all became sinners (1 Corinthians 15).

Did God destroy the earth?

Yes, He did, but He also restored it with the opportunity to worship. In addition to salvation, worship has a restorative quality that reminds us of our rightful place in the bosom of God; we are His beloved. He cherishes every one of us and wants us close to His bosom.

Romans 12:1 (NKJV) —

> "I beseech you therefore, brethren, by the mercies of God, that you present your bodies a living sacrifice, holy, acceptable to God, which is your reasonable service."

This is our reasonable service in this dispensation of grace we are in. God does not want the bull, the ox, the goat, or the dove. Grace has been extended to all mankind, all who believe, all who put their trust in Him, and now the acceptable, desirable sacrifice is you (Colossians 1:21-22).

So, if you believe that you are undone and fragmented, know that God will love every one of your broken pieces and put you back together as you live a life of worship. If you believe you are unqualified because of what you did last summer, last night, or moments ago, know that nothing can separate you from God's love. Not one thing is more powerful than God's decision to remain in love with you. Keep in mind that God showed you His love first before asking you for anything.

1 John 4:10 (NKJV) —

> "Herein is love, not that we loved God, but that he loved us, and sent his Son to be the propitiation for our sins."

1 John 4:19 (NKJV) —

> "We love him, because he first loved us."

His love was present before you were born which means you were born into God's love as a permanent fixture. How powerful is that? How unbeatable is that? How remarkable is that? How unfailing is that? There's a song I am in love with by Maverick City that says, "I'll never be more loved than I am right now. I wasn't holding you up so there's nothing I could do to let you down."

The revelation that brought forth that song is the idea that out of His love came our existence, our restoration, and direction for our future. Do not allow misaligned thoughts to lead you into hiding like Adam. But even if you choose to hide, He will come after you. That's how much you are desired by God. It wasn't possible for your performance to be rewarded with God's love because God's love appeared before you first opened your eyes. God's love draws us in and gives us the opportunity to learn, to grow, to pass, and fail tests without the fear of ever being abandoned or rejected. God is not the unfair father or the unfair mother that neglects the child she bears. You are never forgotten by Him. His thoughts toward you are endless, even when you think very little of yourself. Condemnation is the script of religion, not the face of Christ Jesus. Do we have a responsibility to walk according to the Word, apply faith in God to our lives, and allow the power of His Word to cleanse and correct our behaviors?

Absolutely.

Yes, grace covers our sin. However, grace also influences our hearts to be conformed to the image of Christ in every area. Conformity takes place in our pursuit of God. Condemnation will never produce conformity, but submission inevitably will. Submission, repentance, brokenness, and confession characterize the life of the believer and the heart of a worshipper. Each of those elements is compounded to produce a fragrant aroma that brings pleasure to God. David was a lying fornicator, yet God made him king because in his heart was worship. Moses was a fearful, stuttering, insecure man yet God equipped him to lead Israel because in his heart he found worship. Joseph was a prideful, bragging, immature young man yet God let him lead his entire family because in his heart he found worship. Abraham almost gave his whole wife away to a man that did not know God, yet the Lord led him into promise because in his heart he found worship. Rahab was a harlot, and yet God saved her because in her heart He found worship. It will never be that your greatest successes redeem you from your sinful nature that will at times betray you. You will be rewarded by God because of where your faith will lead you in Him. May your faith lead and guide you perpetually into His presence. May you never deny yourself the beauty of His holiness because you misperceive that your action or inaction renders you unqualified to draw near. His perfecting blood and the reconciliation accompanying your trust in the cross has perfected you once and for all in Him. You are not presented to the Father of glory in your own self; you are presented to the Father in Christ Jesus (Hebrews 10:6-10).

It was the will of Christ Jesus to become your perfection by way of the cross that He bore. Your perfection is not only unattainable, but it is unnecessary.

Hallelujah!

You have been sanctified through the offering of the body of Jesus Christ, once and for all (Hebrews 10:10). You have been perfected forever by His sacrifice. Our life on this side reflects a willingness and cooperation with His ways being worked out in us. Where the Bible says to work out your soul salvation with fear and trembling, in Philippians 2:12, He is saying to cooperate with and apply the cleansing, redeeming, perfecting Word of God to our life in a way that yields His character, integrity, and love. We do this in reverence, which is a holy fear, not an unhealthy fear of God. It is because we trust in His ways that we submit ourselves to Him. It is not because we fear rejection, abandonment, or forsaking, for our God does not forsake. In Him, you are His forever.

One of the most trying times of my life beyond my term of imprisonment was the horrid abuse I endured under the leadership of a pastor that called me daughter. Lies, persecutions, scandals, and blatant disrespect riddled the relationship I thought would bring a degree of maturity to my infancy. Rejection, my strong man, debilitated the growth of my soul as a young woman because of my misperception of fatherhood. I came to understand that the intention of the enemy in the abuse I endured was to distort my perception of Abba Father. This would have prevented me from pursuing perfect daughterhood because I did not experience perfect fatherhood. It was in worship, times of surrender, when I cast down the burdens of my soul, that God revealed this to me. Rejection is the enemy's tool against the beloved of God. Rejection was Satan's tactic to keep me away from the Father that loved me. Rejection is a lie in and of itself. It was in worship where I would ball up in pain and cry out to God. There, He answered me.

A part of me, the deeper part of my spirit, was untouched by the mistreatment. I had never undergone such a thing. I had never been lied on so many times, not even in my childhood, but I realized it was actually the father of lies using my "spiritual father" as a tool. Our warfare is never with human flesh. Our warfare is only with the enemy of God which is the devil.

Ephesians 6:12 (NKJV) —

"For we do not wrestle against flesh and blood, but against principalities, against powers, against the rulers of the darkness of this age, against spiritual hosts of wickedness in the heavenly places."

No war existed between my pastor, his influencer, and me. The only warfare I withstood was against the enemy wanting to rob me of the enjoyment of Abba's covering. My former leader was a pastor of pastors, a leader of leaders, and had a tremendous heart for this generation. He was an amazing teacher of the gospel and was for the things of the kingdom. Despite his influence against me, he was the beloved of God, too.

I committed myself to prayer, fasting, and passion-filled worship, and the Lord changed my mind and heart for this man as well as those influencing his abuse in ways you may not believe. I would pray until I fell in love with my abuser, and by falling in love I mean in the most healthy, holy way. I not only saw myself as a victim of an attack but saw my former leaders as victims of an attack also. I could not allow the lack of consistent, safe leadership to dissuade me from believing that God is a perfect Father. I see why the enemy thought he would win. I had not known a father as Father.

The first time I was introduced to fatherhood in the kingdom was by amazing, anointed, gifted men of God that turned around and rendered rejection as my natural father did. The enemy thought he would trap me with disbelief, leading to unbelief, but I learned as a disciple of the Word that the devil does nothing but lie, even if he uses the truth to communicate it. Was I abused by male leaders in the church that I anticipated love from?

Absolutely.

Like He did with the first man, Adam, that sinned, God sent me another of a more kingdom-made stature. Jesus is referred to as the Second Man, the One whose righteousness undid the work of his unrighteous predecessor. Well, our heavenly Father knew I needed safe spiritual fatherhood. In the face of the abuse, neglect, and mishandling I described, He sent me another. As a matter of fact, He sent me two. To this day, I remain accountable and fathered dearly by two outstanding citizens of the kingdom that absolutely love God and walk in the ways of His kingdom. Sometimes, leadership and agape love won't come from the heart you expect to cover you, but they will come from a conduit of God. Instead of embracing and internalizing rejection from mortal men, I looked to where I was accepted instead.

Did the love that led former fathers to reject me or indicate and define God's true love?

Absolutely not.

During that hard season, God shined His light in every dark way, and He led me with love into a safe place in Him. The love of God is pure and always pure. The ways of man are not. I would have slighted myself had I continued to allow rejection to disciple me away from the Father's embrace. The bosom of Abba is where I belong. This was where He called me. I replaced the longing for an earthly father with my longing for my heavenly Father and pursued His affirmation in the Word of God and worship. Jesus granted me access and boldness and intended to use it in every opportunity I had.

Hebrews 4:16 (NKJV) —

"Let us therefore come boldly unto the throne of grace, that we may obtain mercy, and find grace to help in time of need."

Don't just draw near. Draw near boldly, knowing that whatever help or mercy you need will be found in His presence. God is not just a King seated on a throne in heaven. He is also your personal Perfector. Anything and everything wrong with you and in you, He has positioned Himself to cover and perfect forever.

Chapter Seven

FINDING REST IN WORSHIP

In worship, we find rest. The Bible promises us rest for our weary souls. Jeremiah 31:25 (NKJV) tells us, *"For I have given rest to the weary and joy to the sorrowing."* Worship is the place of rest, a desirable place.

Psalm 23:2 (NKJV) —

> *"He makes me to lie down in green pastures; He leads me beside the still waters."*

Rest is a promise. We really need to regard it as an honorable thing because the Bible describes generations before us missing the rest that was announced. They did not enter in it because the words they heard were not mixed with faith. They were promised rest but died or lived outside of rest because they lacked faith and disobeyed God.

Rest is a tool.

Rest is a weapon.

For in rest, we are reprieved of the labor required to make things happen in the world around us. We are reprieved of the requirement to perform to achieve. See, in God, we live, move, and have our being. What that means on the natural side of things is that we are empowered, or divinely influenced for good works, so that the good works we do are not done in vain. Instead, they perform, excel, and prosper, along with our intention. That can be for spiritual things or natural things. Not all natural things are carnal. There is a difference between naturality and carnality. There's a natural side of life that God wants us not only to enjoy but to thrive in.

3 John 1:2 (NKJV) —

> *"Beloved, I pray that you may prosper in all things and be in health, just as your soul prospers."*

As our soul prospers is what it says. A requirement for the prosperity of the soul is rest. Imagine working 24 hours a day, seven days a week. You cannot wait to get off work on Friday. You cannot wait until the school semester is over for your three to four-month break. You can't wait to have time for yourself. Well, God can't wait to have time with you! The time that He wants with us doesn't always and only look like prayer and worship, lifted hands, and reading our Bible, although all of those things should be a part of our daily lives. The thing is, God walks with you, and He is in you. He is in your daily living and daily moving. He is in the breakfast you prepare. He is the nutrition that fuels your body to endure the day. I remember when this revelation came to me that God is with me wherever I go, as the Bible says in Joshua 1:9 (NKJV) —

> *"Have I not commanded you? Be strong and of good courage; do not be afraid, nor be dismayed, for the Lord your God is with you wherever you go."*

I went through a time of busyness when I thought I was denying God. I felt like I had fallen off. I thought that God was displeased because I went from six to eight hours in worship, devotion, and prayer with Him in the mornings to one hour or two in the season when I was building my business. I became so busy with life. I felt as though I diminished God's presence by showing He was less valuable than the agenda of the day. One day, He spoke to me and said, "I am the greatest part of you. I am the most excellent part of you, and I am not made smaller because the time you devote to me becomes minimal. I am God. I am the biggest thing in your life."

He understands that on the natural side of life, we get busy. He knows that you have responsibilities to perform daily, whether you are a mother, father, employee, member of a team, member of a ministry, leader of a church, or the owner of a business. You have more things to do than read your Bible. God says to delight yourself *also* in Him and He will give you the desires of your heart (Psalm 37:4). He doesn't say delight yourself *only* in Him. He created the world and everything in it for the enjoyment of man in natural life. I don't know where we get the idea that the only things God cares about are the supernatural elements of God, the realms of heaven, and the high-minded things of God. When He says that He will perfect the things that concern you, He must be talking about things on this side of life because, in heaven, the trials of this life are not allowed. There is no sickness and disease, and there is no contention or rivalry. There are no trials and tribulations in heaven. So, even in the requirements of our daily living, God wants us to give Him access.

By profession, I am a hairstylist. I understand that God has given me creativity, but I am careful not to take ownership or authorship of creativity. He who created the heavens and the earth is the Creator, and He created me to create. As a hairstylist, there are some complex haircuts I want to execute. I remember that God told me, "Let Me come into that. Make room for Me in your execution, and watch My creative grace implode in your hands." I would have dreams of different hairstyles, ponytails, and haircuts, and I would perform them according to the grace that God gifted me to create them. I was perfecting pixie cuts with face-framing features in the '90s when people weren't doing that, and I have evidence to prove it. I was shaping faces with coils and waves before it became the hot thing that it is today. I would envision ponytails and styles, and I'd call my Godsister so that I could do the styles I envisioned on her that I had not seen done before.

When it was time for Jacob to separate from Laban, did you see Jacob laboring for the ideas that increased his wealth? The creative ingenuity imparted into Jacob that created the wealth he would live by came through rest, not his labor. Jacob lived a life devoted to appreciating the provision of God. In his worship of and to the God that provided for him and walked with him, Jacob decided to give God a tenth of his earnings.

Genesis 28:20-23 (NKJV) —

> *"Then Jacob made a vow, saying, 'If God will be with me, and keep me in this way that I am going, and give me bread to eat and clothing to put on, so that I come back to my father's house in peace, then the Lord shall be my God. And this stone which I have set as a pillar shall be God's house, and of all that You give me I will surely give a tenth to You.'"*

The tithe was not prescribed to us through the law. I have taught that tithing is an act of worship because worship is the fruit of trusting God. Tithing is a manifestation of our trust in God with our money, just like offering yourself to God as a living sacrifice is a manifestation of trusting God with your life. Jacob gave God a tenth of everything given to him.

How did Jacob know to do that?

No one instructed Jacob to do that. We don't see any reports of scribes detailing how Abraham did the same thing when he tithed to Melchizedek, a priest after the order of Christ the Messiah.

Rest can be equated to our reliance on God. Reliance upon God makes room for miracles. Miracles do not require human strength, but they are performed by God's supernatural power. It isn't that He is calling us to inactivity; that's not the rest He authors. God does not condone laziness. Instead, our activity is God-breathed.

In times of rest and refreshing, God will download strategies that we would reject during times of busyness or worry. Jacob could not have endured the hardship nor the abuse and manipulation of Laban while maintaining a Godly composure unless he made time to rest, hear, regroup, and be refreshed in God. We see two times in scripture where Jacob received what he needed from God as he rested.

Genesis 28:11 (NKJV) —

> "So he came to a certain place and stayed there all night, because the sun had set. And he took one of the stones of that place and put it at his head, and he lay down in that place to sleep. Then he dreamed, and behold, a ladder was set up on the earth, and its top reached to heaven; and there the angels of God were ascending and descending on it. And behold, the Lord stood above it and said: 'I am the Lord God of Abraham your father and the God of Isaac; the land on which you lie I will give to you and your descendants. Also your descendants shall be as the dust of the earth; you shall spread abroad to the west and the east, to the north and the south; and in you and in your seed all the families of the earth shall be blessed. Behold, I am with you and will keep you wherever you go, and will bring you back to this land; for I will not leave you until I have done what I have spoken to you.'"

Genesis 32:24 (NKJV) —

> "Then Jacob was left alone; and a Man wrestled with him until the breaking of day."

If there was ever a moment for Jacob to fall into discouragement, it was interrupted when he laid down to rest. God's instruction, His presence, and His word simply met him and gave him what was needed for the next leg of his journey. Angels spoke to Jacob in dreams and met with him when he would draw away to be alone with the Lord. Jacob was acquainted with God; his walk with Him was a lifestyle. He was always cognizant of the presence of God even amid adversity.

Genesis 31:5 (NKJV) —

> "...and said to them, 'I see your father's countenance, that it is not favorable toward me as before; but the God of my father has been with me.'"

We believe and have been led to understand that the only way our provision comes is through work. But I say unto you, by the wisdom of God and the Word backing me, that provision comes to you through your worship, and there is a part of your worship that applies the gift God gave you to perform or to execute a skill needed in the workplace or marketplace. In other words, yes, your gift will bring income; it is designed to be that way. There is a part of worship that will require your work, and there is a part of worship that will release the reward of work you will not have to perform.

Hebrews 4:11 (NKJV) —

> "Let us therefore be diligent to enter that rest, lest anyone fall according to the same example of disobedience. "

In another translation, it reads —

> "Let us therefore labor to enter this rest, lest anyone fall according to the same example of disobedience."

The word "labor" does not mean toil; it means to have earnest intention to enter the rest made available to us in God. The fourth chapter of the book of Hebrews describes a rest that became available to us when the worlds were made. So, this is not a rest that comes to you because you perform for God. It is a rest that was made available to you because God knew rest was needed, and rest was what God Himself experienced on the last day of creation. Let me explain that further.

Hebrews 4:1 (NKJV) —

> "Therefore, since a promise remains of entering His rest, let us fear lest any of you seem to have come short of it."

God does not want us to come short of the benefit of worship, which is rest.

Hebrews 4:2 (NKJV) —

> "For indeed the gospel was preached to us as well as to them; but the word which they heard did not profit them, not being mixed with faith in those who heard it."

This is what I said earlier. Let's look at both verses in the New Living Translation —

> "God's promise of entering his rest still stands, so we ought to tremble with fear that some of you might fail to experience it. For this good news – that God has prepared this rest – has been announced to us just as it was to them. But it did them no good because they didn't share the faith of those who listened to God."

Saints, rest is available to you now. I prophesy to you. I speak into your weary soul, and I say to you that your days of toiling are over. Your days of trying to figure out the next day of your life are over. The Bible says to be anxious for nothing but in all things you are to give thanks. Give thanks for what you've been given, and give thanks for what you're aware of came from God. Open your eyes and see that there is plenty all around you. David commanded his soul to bless the Lord in the middle of turmoil, trial, and warfare.

Why?

Because his soul needed a reminder of what he had already been given. His soul needed a reminder that he was already in an abundance of something that his perspective led him to believe he lost. He took his eye off the God that walked the sea and put his eye on the storm. David commanded his soul to bless the Lord when warfare was all around him and when enemies came upon him to eat up his flesh. I say unto you, that no longer will you see your warfare bigger than the God of your victory. No longer will you see your lowly place greater than the heavenly place you have been seated in. God has made rest available to you, and according to the Word of God, His rest still stands. His rest has made a decision to wait for your arrival. Receive His rest today. Receive His rest now in the mighty name of Jesus.

We let life deposit fear in our souls, but we don't reverence the rest that God gives. We don't reverence the idea of missing God because we're walking in fear when God has not given us a spirit of fear but a spirit of power, love, and a sound mind. Therefore, when we walk in fear, we are actively embracing a demonic gift, not fully realizing that we are denying ourselves from inheriting the benefit that God came to give us. We don't reverence freedom from fear enough. The Bible says we ought to tremble with fear at the idea of never actually experiencing the rest that's been made available to us. But no, we're more worried about tomorrow. We're more worried about a bill. We're more worried about who likes us and who speaks to us and who embraces us than we are about losing this honorable place in God called rest.

Back to Hebrews 4. Oh, God. They missed this place of rest because they didn't listen to God.

Verse 3 —

"For only we who believe can enter his rest..."

This rest is for the believer. This rest is not the pretty picture of resting on a hammock on the beach. The rest that we have in God is not just a pretty picture. It is the reality of reliance on a God who cares for us. The latter part of that verse in Hebrews 4:3 says —

"...even though this rest has been ready since he made the world."

We know this rest is ready because of the place in the scriptures where it mentions the seventh day.

Hebrews 4:4 (NKJV) —

"For He has spoken in a certain place of the seventh day in this way: "And God rested on the seventh day from all His works."

Listen to that, the rest that God is speaking of, the rest that God has made available to you and me was made available the day He entered into it Himself. We can now rest because He rested. The scripture says that this rest was made available when the worlds were framed. It says, I repeat, "Although the works were finished from the foundations of the world." The works were finished that constructed the realm of rest for the believer in the book of Genesis the day that God took rest from His work. God, in the time He took to form man in the beginning, was not toiling. The "work" that God performed before resting on the seventh day was performed before toiling became relevant. This work was not like toil; it was more akin to productivity. Toiling did not come until the fall of man, until sin. It was a part of the curse on the natural man that we now have to toil to gain what His rest offered us in worship before the fall. God, after He put forth His efforts to form man, rested from His accomplishments (His creation), and He empowered and equipped us to do the same.

Ephesians 2:10 (NKJV) —

For we are His workmanship, created in Christ Jesus for good works, which God prepared beforehand that we should walk in them."

Hebrews 4:11 (NKJV) —

> *"Let us therefore be diligent to enter that rest, lest anyone fall according to the same example of disobedience."*

If we disobey God, as the people of Israel did, we risk missing the opportunity to enter this rest God has made available to us. I believe this is exactly why there are far too many depressed believers. The number of depressed believers astonishes me, and it's simply because we have not perfected this gift called rest. The idea of rest, established in the peace of mind, understands that God is with us, that God is for us, and everything that could hit us in life pales in comparison to our relationship with God. The Word says in Romans 8:18 (NKJV) —

> *"For I consider that the sufferings of this present time are not worthy to be compared with the glory which shall be revealed in us."*

Some of the glory we're looking to be revealed comes to us now and is not upon our entry to heaven. There's a glory that God wants to reveal to us through trials and the fire of our lives here on earth.

1 Peter 4:12-23 (NKJV) —

> *"Beloved, do not think it strange concerning the fiery trial which is to try you, as though some strange thing happened to you; but rejoice to the extent that you partake of Christ's sufferings, that when His glory is revealed, you may also be glad with exceeding joy."*

1 Peter 1:7 (NKJV) —

> *"That the trial of your faith, being much more precious than of gold that perisheth, though it be tried with fire, might be found unto praise and honour and glory at the appearing of Jesus Christ…"*

The idea of rest and a worry-free life should not simply be characteristic of the elderly who care less about the mundane things of the world. It's for every believer as soon as our perspective shifts.

Why worship?

Because in worship, we find rest.

He says if we disobey as the people of Israel did, we will fall short of this place of rest. In our obedience are green pastures and still waters. Immediately following this admonition in verse 11 of Hebrews 4, we get to verse 12, describing the awesome impact of the Word of God. For years, I have wondered about the relationship between the scripture's discussion of rest flowing directly into the definition or describing the characteristics of the Word of God. He says —

> "For the word of God is living and powerful, and sharper than any two-edged sword, piercing even to the division of soul and spirit, and of joints and marrow, and is a discerner of the thoughts and intents of the heart."

I remember saying to God, "How do You go from discussing rest that's been missed to a people that have failed to enter into it to then describing the Word of God?" I just didn't understand the relationship, and it was today, in His presence, that God showed me that the way to enter rest is His Word.

His Word is a lamp unto our feet and a lamp unto our path. And it is by His Word that the worlds were framed, and if there is enough power in His Word to frame the world, the cosmos, and all things created, then there is enough power in His Word to construct our heart's desire in the atmospheres around us. His Word doesn't just sustain the heavens in which His throne is seated; His Word sustains the very atmospheres, situations, circumstances, changes, needs to be met, and household structures around us. The performing power that your best life requires is found in His Word, not a motivational speech. The source of your encouragement, life spring, well-being, and your lifted countenance is in the power of His Word. His Word encounters impossibility and imparts possibility right into its core. This is why the Word of God says that nothing is impossible for those who believe.

Believe what?

Believe the Word of God because believing the Word of God releases the power of His Word to enact change in the life of the believer. You cannot enter into this rest, into this place of worship, without access that has come through the Word of God revealed, preached, taught, or received. To qualify to be good ground, you must till the soil that receives the seed.

Mark 4:2-9 (NKJV) —

> *"Then He taught them many things by parables, and said to them in His teaching: 'Listen! Behold, a sower went out to sow. And it happened, as he sowed, that some seed fell by the wayside; and the birds of the air came and devoured it. Some fell on stony ground, where it did not have much earth; and immediately it sprang up because it had no depth of earth. But when the sun was up it was scorched, and because it had no root it withered away. And some seed fell among thorns; and the thorns grew up and choked it, and it yielded no crop. But other seed fell on good ground and yielded a crop that sprang up, increased and produced: some thirtyfold, some sixty, and some a hundred.' And He said to them, 'He who has ears to hear, let him hear!'"*

The Bible says you keep the word, and that word "keep" means to manage it. You don't just sit under the teaching of the Word of God, which is as powerful as Hebrews 4:12 describes. You do something with the Word that has been imparted to you. You must do something with the Word that's wanting to perform in and around you. You must cooperate with the performing power of God's Word with obedience and application to your life. I hope you don't leave the jewels and revelations of the Word that I'm presenting to you on the pages of this book on these pages. I pray that the word that is revealed to you in this book becomes a part of your prayer life and structures your days ahead. You must take the Word of God and apply it to the thought life of inner man. In doing so, you will see the Word manifest all around you.

Worship gives rest to the weary soul. It isn't that the Lord won't use the work of your hands. It's that God will bless the work of your hands so that what you do with your hands produces what toiling is incapable of. In worship, you find the rest in God, and rest is available to you because rest is available to God. He can only take us where He's entered into Himself, and the Bible says in Hebrews 4:14 (NKJV) —

> "Seeing then that we have a great High Priest who has passed through the heavens, Jesus the Son of God, let us hold fast our confession. For we do not have a High Priest who cannot sympathize with our weaknesses, but was in all points tempted as we are, yet without sin. Let us therefore come boldly to the throne of grace, that we may obtain mercy and find grace to help and time of need."

What I am saying to you is that the rest available to you in God is where your help resides. You won't find help in your anxiety, in your worry, in despair, and in complaining. You will find help in His presence. And it is not the Word alone that will grant you rest, not this rest. It is the Word that you believe mixed with faith. You have believed yourself into the most Holy Place of God, and I don't care where you're sitting or standing; this place made for you in God follows you wherever you go. That is the beauty of relationship. That is the beauty of walking with God, that your access to Him is always available because He is always near and nearer than you know.

There is a popular worship song I love—"Abba" by Jonathan David Hesler. The words of the song say, "You're more real than the ground I'm standing on. You're more real than the words on my tongue." God is nearer than you know, and the fact that He has given us access to everything of Him and everything from Him tells me that if we find ourselves weary or dizzy by life, it is because our perspective has shifted away from our help. Why do you think that Jesus could remain asleep on a pillow in the middle of a storm?

Mark 4:35-41 (NKJV) —

> "On the same day, when evening had come, He said to them, 'Let us cross over to the other side.' Now when they had left the multitude, they took Him along in the boat as He was. And other little boats were also with Him. And a great windstorm arose, and the waves beat into the boat, so that it was already filling. But He was in the stern, asleep on a pillow. And they awoke Him and said to Him, 'Teacher, do You not care that we are perishing?' Then He arose and rebuked the wind, and said to the sea, 'Peace, be still!' And the wind ceased and there was a great calm. But He said to them, 'Why are you so fearful? How is it that you have no faith?' And they feared exceedingly, and said to one another, 'Who can this be, that even the wind and the sea obey Him!'"

The disciples were being developed, but they had not yet acquired the level of assurance and trust in God that would eventually come to them. They were in the process. So, I say to you, you are in the process. Don't beat yourself up about your process. Don't consider yourself a failure because you're in the process. You're in the process as the disciples were in the process. So, whatever you don't know about God, be excited that He will reveal that side of Himself to you. This is how we walk with God. We ask Him to show us sides of Him that we've not yet seen.

The disciples awoke and were scared because they were looking at the storm and not at the One with the power to calm it. They saw the storm as a weapon against them. Jesus saw the storm as an opportunity to prove His deity. It was not that He had anything to prove, but His demonstration helped those needing to grow in encounter. Christ's demonstration of power became a witness to those who would receive and walk in His power. He used this opportunity to teach those walking with Him and those of us reading the account in scripture how to apply God's power with demonstration.

Jesus was resting when the storm hit. The rest He enjoyed with the comfort of a pillow remained the same as the storm approached, grew stronger, and drew nearer to the ship. The storm did not awaken Him, nor did it unsettle Him. The winds and the rain did not move Him, not for one moment.

Why?

How?

Because His perspective of oneness was not afflicted or impaired by a brewing storm.

We don't have an issue enjoying times of refreshing in God until a storm comes our way. We have learned to walk in peace, but we seem to only maintain peace until adversity strikes. Doubt is a natural response to uncertainty, but it is our responsibility to lay down our doubts. Doubt is rooted in fear and the culprit of our anxiety which is the opposite of rest. Your physical body can be inactive while your heart, mind, and soul feel like they're on a losing battlefield. Isaiah 9:7 (NKJV) teaches us that there shall be no end to our peace —

> "Of the increase of His government and peace there will be no end, Upon the throne of David and over His kingdom, To order it and establish it with judgment and justice From that time forward, even forever. The zeal of the Lord of hosts will perform this."

Galatians 6:15-16 (NKJV) —

> *"For in Christ Jesus neither circumcision nor uncircumcision avails anything, but a new creation. And as many as walk according to this rule, peace and mercy be upon them, and upon the Israel of God."*

And John 14:27 (NKJV) —

> *"Peace I leave with you, My peace I give to you; not as the world gives do I give to you. Let not your heart be troubled, neither let it be afraid."*

Peace, from its Greek root, pronounced "I-rah-nay," is defined as quietness and rest. It actually sounds a lot like "irony," doesn't it? The peace of God, surpassing our understanding, is ironic to the storms of life! What should take us cannot withstand the arm of God covering us during trial. I realized a few years ago that what I experienced every so often were mild forms of anxiety. While living our lives before God, weathering storms, and trying to balance life, fear will try to find its way through our areas of uncertainty. One thing I always tell my team is that life happens and while you don't know what life will bring, it would be to your advantage to be equipped to handle it.

Life happens to us, and not only does our focus shift, but our expectation shifts sometimes as well. The disciples thought they were going to die because they misinterpreted the storm. The storm gave them the opportunity to see the hand of God move against what came to destroy them. Instead of being a tool against them, it was a tool for them. Unmoved while resting, Jesus awakened with the power of rebuke in His mouth, and at His word, the storm ceased. Jesus never lost sight of the nearness of the Father. As such, He never saw Himself without help except during a moment of darkness while He was lifted on the cross and the Father had to turn His back because of the sin His son became for man.

When we take on the mind of Christ, we are renewed into a proper perspective that keeps us at peace in the face of trials and storms. We haven't been given the peace of man, but the literal peace of Jesus Christ as demonstrated in this passage of scripture. As this peace, supernatural in power, kept His mind at bay as peace ruled in His heart, so shall it keep our minds at bay when we keep the proper perspective—that our help is always near.

Peace is what believers need to master. We need to master our place in God and the authority we have been given. What Jesus needed at that moment, He commanded, and it came to pass. There is power to speak life and there is power to enjoy life as we nestle ourselves in worship.

Faith cleanses the lens of the eye and the eye that is good. The Bible says when the eye is good, the body is full of light. When your eye is good and your body is full of light, you walk faith-filled in the face of adversity. You remain faith-filled when challenges present themselves over and over again. You remain in faith, trusting that God is not only able and willing, but that God is with you. He is with you, and where God is present, rest is available. You, son, you, daughter, are now free to find rest in God.

Chapter Eight

THE PRESS AND POWER OF CREATING AN ATMOSPHERE OF WORSHIP

When we gave ourselves to idols and were dead in our sins, the Father decided we were worthy. He created us with significance, and through worship, He expounds on the worth He planted in you. Through worship, He exposes our worth to Him and His worth to us in His drawing near. He doesn't just draw near—He comes to abide with His Presence and His voice, both of which are the change agents of our current conditions. We make room for all His Presence and voice comes to perform in us by resisting our resistance against Him. What I mean by that is we can deny His voice access to our atmosphere by diminishing His voice when He speaks.

Hebrews 3:7-8 (NKJV) —

> "Wherefore (as the Holy Ghost saith, Today if ye will hear his voice, Harden not your hearts, as in the provocation, in the day of temptation in the wilderness."

He will abide in silence if we restrict Him, but He wants to abide with a voice. He wants to abide by manifesting His authority.

Ephesians 3:20 (NKJV) —

"Now to Him who is able to do exceedingly abundantly above all that we ask or think, according to the power that works in us."

He wants to abide in the fullness of His presence so that we may know that relationship with Him is unscarred and unmarked by our feelings or frailties. He wants to abide in us, exposing His love for us, and disposing of all our feelings of unworthiness. He not only reveals to us through His nearness that He finds us worthy, but He reveals sides of Him that display His worthiness. God is trustworthy and credible. We can trust Him with our entire being and the surrender of our entire lives. That does not negate the natural side of living that we enjoy. We need not see God in the way of our pleasure, in the way of our advancement, or in the way of our elevation. But God is the way to our elevation. He is the way to our expansion. He is the way to our pleasure, for God created us and He created everything around us for our pleasure.

Genesis 2:9 (NKJV) —

"And out of the ground the Lord God made every tree grow that is pleasant to the sight and good for food."

God authors pleasure. It is the enemy who perverts pleasure. God has given pleasure to man to satisfy our souls. When we open our eyes and see life through the lens of God, we will see abundance before us, not restriction.

Religion opposes the freedom that God gives and reveals. What Christ gives is abundance. Through time in His presence, we learn God through fellowship. The precious moments in God's presence continue to add value to our lives. Worship gives us the opportunity to see life through the lens of God and to do life through the lens of God. In worship, we invite the fullness of God to perform in us, around us, and for us, according to His perfect will. It gets no better than that! In worship, we surrender our fight and our labor. In worship, we surrender our labor by allowing the King of Glory to perform work that does not require our hands. This does not mean that we retire at the age of 25 or 32 or that we retire at the age of our salvation. What it means is that we have a voice and a light that lead us on the pathway to make destiny easier to attain.

My life is a reflection of moving when I hear God speak. Yes, I am a leader, and yes, God has called me to pioneer. Yes, God has made me ambitious and formidable, and He has given me the fortitude to outlast many. He has given me the strength and power of an overcomer, all of which reflects the character of Jesus. The instructions God gave to my spirit man in Genesis 1 in proportion with the call of God on my life are reflected in my personality and work ethic.

Genesis 1:27-28 (NKJV) —

> "So God created man in His own image; in the image of God He created him; male and female He created them. Then God blessed them, and God said to them, 'Be fruitful and multiply; fill the earth and subdue it; have dominion over the fish of the sea, over the birds of the air, and over every living thing that moves on the earth.'"

I am ambitious because He has given me instruction for purpose's sake. I walk in the authority to reproduce and enter into dominion. I don't go after what I see in a carnal way led by selfish ambition or a desire to be seen. I go after what He reveals to me through His spirit, and because I go after the revealed thing, He helps me to attain it. His promises are set in place, and through continual pursuit, I walk into what He has awaiting my arrival at its appointed time. People have told me for years to go forth in ministry, host a conference, and lead a team. I refused. I move by the unction of Holy Spirit, endeavoring to keep pace with His timing.

Many people are living their lives, going after the dreams of the ones they envy and going after dreams fueled by jealousy, contention, and strife.

And guess what?

They will get it because there is another god that offers a form of godliness. There is another god that offers a form of acceleration. There is another god that offers a form of elevation, but their route is dark. They don't care what source they thrive off of because they only care about their end goal. I care about the source of my encouragement to go forth because it's the purity of the instruction that will sustain me. It is the purity of the motive behind the work that will thrust me forth in God and bring glory to His name. If you build on a faulty foundation, what you build will fall when the storms come, the rains fall, and the winds blow. What is built on the Rock, who is Jesus, will remain.

Did you know that Jesus builds more than churches? Did you know that Jesus builds more than ministries? Jesus builds the countenances that become the rock from which your family is fed. Jesus builds pillars of our communities who become bridges to greater communities. Jesus is the extract. He is the component of strength of the builder of all things. He will even build your esteem. Did you know that your esteem matters to Him just as much as a church building, a work of ministry, or a business? He builds in you in times of worship when you build on Him. You build on Him through a lifestyle of worship. You surrender all of your doings to the One who will instruct you for advancement. God knows the end from the beginning, and He is the author of not just good gifts but perfect gifts.

You have been created for good works. When you perform from the place of grace, your work will last. It will be sustained, and your help will come. I do not say to you that because you live a life of worship, your life will be made easy. That would be a lie. For *"those who suffer with Him also reign with Him"* (2 Timothy 2:12 NKJV). There is a relationship between reigning and suffering that believers must understand. God never promised us a bed of roses. God never promised us a life without obstacles. He promised us victory over obstacles. He always causes us to triumph. You see your victory, even when the circumstance doesn't change, if you begin to see God as a circumstance changer and not a countenance builder; you will make an idol out of His performing power. God Himself is worth our surrender whether our circumstances change or not. He doesn't become worth your worship, surrender, or life because He does things for you, opens doors for you, connects you to people you want to be connected to, or because He meets your needs. God is worthy of worship because He is the only one enthroned. He is worthy of worship simply because He is God. Because of your worship, His hand will move on your behalf; He will war on your behalf; He will annihilate warfare. He will undo the work of devils on your behalf. He will show you favor. Yes, He will grant you opportunities, but He's not worth your worship because of what He does. He is worth your worship because of who He is and who He revealed Himself to be to you. He is God, fundamental to everything. He showed Himself to you. And because He showed Himself to you, He is worth your worship.

There are many whose eyes remain blinded by the god of this world who cannot see Him. But you see Him. It is a privilege for you to even know that He is God. He is eternally God, He is uncreated, and His throne shall not be moved. I dare you to worship the Lord your God in the deepest places of your darkness, in the lowest moments of your life. I dare you to surrender the weight of the world that you continue to bear on your shoulders. I dare you to surrender it to God. He says, "Take my yoke upon you for my yoke is easy, and my burden is light." He says, "Cast every care before me, for I, the Lord care for you. And I God will perfect those things which concern you." His perfection won't always look like an immediate turnaround. Sometimes, it may not be immediate, but His perfection will first perform in you. By perfection in you, I mean that He will bring you to a place of maturity where natural circumstances matter less. Then, He will give you a circumstance that He can trust you to steward and still give Him the glory. If He answers you quickly, how soon would you walk away? Whoa, but in worship, He will conform you to the image of His Son made to sleep through the storm. He will grant you a peace that surpasses all understanding, and in worship, you will know Him by name, and you will know Him by His presence.

I remember when I had to undergo a very dark time in my life. Oh, God, it felt like pain was waiting for me to open my eyes in the morning. It felt like pain had crept itself into the pillow that I laid my head on. I had undergone a time of intense and destructive spiritual abuse by former leaders and sisters in Christ that left me depleted and feeling defeated. I was persecuted and lied on, even put out of a church that was once held in my living room. Following this, I joined another house that was later heavily influenced by a Jezebelic spirit. This spirit unleashed lies that lead to undeserving persecution, mocking, and slander. The enemy was trying to get me to rehearse rejection while the Lord was grooming me in humility during my times of worship.

I would be awakened at dawn because there was something in me that was greater than my pain. It was a desire to see God show up in me and for me in my times of need. I would awaken early in the mornings. It got to a point where I was so hungry for God that 6 a.m. wasn't early enough anymore. And before I knew it, 5 a.m. was no longer early enough. And then 4 a.m. was no longer early enough. So, I began waking up at 3:30 a.m. to begin seeking Him. This was when I started drinking coffee. I would go into the basement of my empty house that I had just moved into that I was unable to fill due to the economic crash of 2008. I listened to the rhema Word of the Lord. Holy Spirit told me to make my home an altar. I would walk my floor in the presence of God. I would pray until the Holy Ghost prayed through me. I would release my language to God until the Lord took over my tongue. I would open my mouth and wouldn't lift my voice in English until the Spirit of God gave me language. In those times, He gave me the language of the victorious. He gave me the language of the one whose head would be lifted high. He gave me the language of the one who walked under the anointing of King Cyrus to break iron gates and unblock barriers before me. He gave me the language of the one who would land on hind's feet in high places even when life brought me low. He gave me authority over darkness as I surrendered my darkness to Him. I learned what it felt like and what it meant to bear the burden of the Lord and the yoke of God, which He says is easier to bear than tribulation. I entered into His presence with boldness and expectation. I grew to understand that what I was called to carry was the "burden," or weight of His glory, which would at times feel like suffering. A person's yes, or access, or money, or acceptance, or honor began to make much less of a difference in my life. With a kingdom perspective, I looked to God, not man.

Don't get me wrong. We need people. Moreover, we need the people of God set in place to be conduits of the Father. But when those folks fail us, we are not lost or without help. The One authorizing their assignment to you will ensure the work is completed. The kingdom of God is much larger than some leaders will ever preach. Healed and in wholeness, I looked for the God-factor in my leaders over and above their human frailty to prevent my gaze from being fragmented by offense. It was the glory of God revealed to me in pain, trauma, tribulation, and trial that made remarkable change.

I remember the day that I went into my basement at 3:30 am. I went down, left the lights off, and sat in His presence until He showed up. I set myself in agreement to pray into His presence. I am reminded of Jacob, who the Bible describes as one who wrestled with God. He didn't wrestle against God because no man wrestles against God and wins. But he wrestled with God. He postured himself boldly before the throne of grace to get the help he needed, which was found in God's presence. I sat in silence, growing in confidence. I remained still until the glorious light of Christ appeared before me in an open vision. In weakness, confusion, despair, and discouragement, God sent me His light. My life had become its own sign and wonder. What I endured made me greater on the inside.

I admonish you today that all the help you need is in worship. All the help you need is bound in the hope of glory. His name is Jesus. His power is expressed by way of Holy Spirit who abides in every believer and draws near to the broken, to the one that cries out to Him in need.

That morning, the Lord showed me light, literal light in the Spirit. And I know that God gave me a glimpse of glory to keep me. And in the moment when God revealed His glory to me in darkness, I understood that the pain I experienced matters so little in comparison to the glory I gained through suffering with Christ. This is not a word of depression. This is not a word that should discourage the saints. No one is looking forward to anguish. Not even Jesus looked forward to anguish. He said to the Father in the garden, "If this cup could pass from Me, take it, but nevertheless, not My will, but Your will be done" because He understood the purpose of the pain in His life. Isaiah 53:10 helps us keep perspective of certain traumas that come when it says, *"Yet it pleased the Lord to bruise Him."*

Many of you reading this, many of those in the Body of Christ, and those outside of the body of Christ have been offended out of God's presence. Because you're offended, you are deterred from pursuing the presence of God. You are offended that He didn't answer you or did not answer you the way you wanted Him to answer you. You are offended that He did not perform for you the way that you wanted Him to perform for you. But God says, "How dare you to be offended at Me when all that I give you is perfect. Even what I allow you to endure serves a perfect purpose. It all works together for your good."

When you look at the account of Job, you will see that God gave Satan access to afflict Job's belongings, but not Job's life. If you count all Job lost as your frame of reference, you will see the wrong thing. God gave Satan access to Job, knowing that Job would withstand the trial. The access God gave held a mystery to be revealed to Satan that those that belong to God will remain in faith. What tribulation God allowed proved Job's significance to God and God's significance to Job. This is a message our lives need to preach to the devil: I will not be moved.

It wasn't about what Job had lost, for what God opened the gates for the enemy to take from Job is what God provided in the first place. And how dare any receiver of good and perfect gifts, or any receiver of the abundance of God, think that God can't restore what He allows an enemy to steal. Shift your perspective as you see the risen Savior writing the story of your life, not just now but for all eternity. What God allowed the enemy to do further proved God's vindication and Job's life.

At the end of the story, God gave Job double for his trouble, and even in that, your eyes should not be on the natural. It's not about how much money you will lose or gain, how much leverage you'll lose or gain, how your bank account will fluctuate, or how God will meet every need. He is able to supply all of your needs according to His riches and glory. But God meets the need beneath the need. He meets the needs of your fragmented soul with His presence.

And I say unto you that more than another business deal, a larger bank account, or the job that will pay six or seven figures, you will need God at work in your inner man. The inward work He performs exceeds the value of diamonds and rubies. Your inner man is frail, weak, and filthy. Your inner man needs God. So what if God makes you a leader of leaders and elevates you above those that hate you and that hated on you and your heart be not clean? How good will you be to glorify Him? How good will you be to those around you? If you consume the victuals that God wants to give you in this season, and you take ownership of your gifts and call yourself great, how good will you be in His eyes? If you discharge God's presence by running away from Him in offense instead of running toward Him. How will you be helped?

We serve a God who neither sleeps nor slumbers. You serve a God that watches over you to perform the work that He has spoken over you and in you. He wants you to prosper internally and externally. The atmosphere that will miss nothing in the path made plain before you is that of worship. The way to water the seed of God's Word and be trusted with more is through worship. The way to be healed from the stony ground or thorny ground of your heart is to worship. The atmosphere required to war off demonic activity, demons, witches, and curses sent your way is worship. God performs not only on your behalf, but He also works against those that work against His will in your life. The atmosphere required to continually and perpetually fuel the cycle of His provision of His presence, His power, and His performance in your life is an atmosphere of worship.

God desires you now as the living sacrifice. Not only are you worthy, but you are required. May His fire meet you right where you are. You are a living, breathing, walking altar. And God's covenant is to meet you every time you call on His name. You will never lose and surrender to God. But in God, you will gain everything on this side of life as well as eternity. God bless you, saints. Walk with God, and He will walk with you.

Chapter Nine

WORSHIP – THE MOST INTIMATE CONNECTION HAPPENS HERE

Your induction into the kingdom of God by way of salvation is immediate. Every benefit of salvation begins the moment you confess with your mouth and believe with your heart that Christ is Lord. At that moment, you are quickened, made alive with Christ Jesus, and you inherit the eternal position of heaven, being seated in heavenly places.

Ephesians 2:5 (NKJV) —

> "Even when we were dead in sins, hath quickened us together with Christ, (by grace ye are saved;)

Ephesians 2:6 (NKJV) —

> "And hath raised us up together, and made us sit together in heavenly places in Christ Jesus."

To be "quickened" is to be co-joined or made alive with Christ. Not only are we internally and spiritually connected with Christ, but we are seated in heavenly places with Him, too. Although your body in its natural state resides here, it is only for a time. One of the beauties of our walk with God lies in the opportunity given us to connect the heavenly realm we are seated in into the natural realm we wake up to morning by morning.

If you used miles, yards, or inches to calculate the distance between your current location and the Father's throne, you may be misled to believe that His tangible presence is an impossibility. To cover the distance, He has brought you a dimension of glory that remains in you and with you forever. This glory, in the form of the Holy Spirit, diminishes the gap and has made nearness your option 24 hours a day. You will not always feel near and will not always believe you are near; however, your thoughts do not negate the new life that your new birth has granted you. If you have confessed the prayer of salvation with conviction and sincerity, you and God are now one and His nearness is your eternal inheritance.

John 15:4 (NKJV) —

> *"Abide in me, and I in you. As the branch cannot bear fruit of itself, except it abide in the vine; no more can ye, except ye abide in me."*

In the above verse, the Greek word for abide is menō, pronounced *men'-o*, and it means "to *stay* (in a given place, state, relation or expectancy) - abide, continue, dwell, endure, be present."

The word "abide" in this context of scripture is literal, not figurative. Holy Spirit, the express person, livelihood, voice, and existence of Jesus Christ, now lives in you in spirit form. You host the Spirit of God inside. You are now His very own temple, and He is now your very own God.

1 Corinthians 3:16 (NKJV) —

> *"Do you not know that you are the temple of God and that the Spirit of God dwells in you?"*

Your connection is not only eternal but internal. When the Father reveals His will for you by way of vision, impression, or unction, He reveals it to Holy Spirit abiding in you. When the preached word comes alive performing something on the inside of you that prevents you from remaining still or silent, it is because the abiding Spirit of God has recognized oneness in the atmosphere. Agreement takes place when the Holy Spirit dwelling in you recognizes the voice of the Father in heaven. That collision, called your inner witness, is often accompanied by a memorable feeling, physical response, or shout.

He gave us His spirit so that we would know Him inwardly and intimately. The Lord wants us to experience Him across all dimensions. His reach extends far beyond intellect and physical sensation. His targets are our hearts, minds, and souls. I sense such an amazing strategy in His pattern.

God could have established a relationship with us however He chose, and it would have sufficed. He is perfect in every way possible. I believe He chose to plant His Spirit deep in our innermost being to outshine everything hidden there. I love when the Lord reveals my heart to me! It has been my prayer from the beginning:

> Make me to know the inner workings of my heart. Father, reveal the secrets within that are layered with pain and masked by accomplishment. Show me the ugliest parts of me and the source of it all, Lord. I don't want an eye to see in others what I cannot see in myself!

We must pray such as that prayer so that we are not blinded by our comfort. We must give ourselves to the cleansing power of the Word that is not repelled by what it exposes. The Word and worship become an internal surgical room to the places in us where healing is most needed.

The heart and soul host the impact of our life experiences—the good, bad, and the ugly. The mind is the battlefield and is too often our greatest hindrance to growing in God. We subject the beautiful power of the mind He gave us to thought patterns preventing us from walking in faith. The soul is the seat of the mind, will, and emotions, having been defined or cultivated by personal experience. As such, the state of our inner man outside of Christ is not only wretched and unclean due to our sinful nature, but it is imperfect, tainted, and tarnished by our life itself.

If I could turn back the hands of time and contribute to my newborn years, it most certainly would have my birth father affixed to our family. I did not volunteer for his abandonment or neglect which led to insecurity and its many branches. My mother walked away due to his infidelity, but his decision not to restore relationship with his children was his own. She never spoke ill of him at all. Not once.

Early in my salvation, I looked to God to understand my poor choices in men and progressive promiscuity. In the gym, while on the elliptical machine, Holy Spirit revealed to me that the root of all I questioned was abandonment. Again, rejection was my strong man. He began to teach me how the neglect I internalized was rooted in fear and how orphanhood matured in me despite having an amazing mother.

It is said by therapists that we stop maturing at the age we are hit with trauma. I have heard it taught by professionals that although we gain age, size, and experiences, a portion of our internal state remains underdeveloped until the trauma is tackled. For years, I housed that broken little girl who wondered why her father didn't want her. For years, my heart was counseled by what I understood a father's desertion to speak - that I was unworthy. My underdeveloped mind and wounded soul sought what my birth father never gave me. I went after affirmation in men which led to a life of whoredom that I must speak about freely.

Was that all I was?

Absolutely not.

There were always admirable qualities about me, but none negated the sting to my soul brought on by this reality.

Unfortunately, there is nothing we can do about the life we're born into; however, our new life of worship can undo the damage if we remain in the abiding place. This is my life's story. God is continually healing me. Worship saved my life.

Some purport that you can heal yourself from such tarnishments. Some advocate self-help books or self-healing methods. Others promote unbiblical or unauthorized methods of healing such as what is offered by way of "spiritual healers," chakra readings, hypnotism, etc. to identify your points of internal pain to be made whole. The Word teaches that God is a healer. The author of and access point to our healing is Jesus Christ Himself. As the scriptures explicitly state, "...by His stripes we are healed."

Isaiah 53:5 (AMPC) —

> "But He was wounded for our transgressions, bruised for our guilt and iniquities. The chastisement [needful to obtain] peace and well-being for us was upon Him, and with the stripes [that wounded] Him, we are healed and made whole."

He took the punishment, and that made us whole. Through his bruises, we get healed. To seek spiritists for what He endured suffering to get to us is dishonorable, to say the least.

Healing in Hebrew is defined as "râphâh," pronounced "raw-faw," which means "to mend (by stitching), cure (cause to) heal, physician, repair, thoroughly make whole" (Strong's Concordance H7495). We call Him Jehovah Raphah because Jesus is the healer of the worshipper's wounds. The Lord has healed my broken heart from the fatherlessness of my days in the womb to the betrayals of last month. The healing properties of the body that cause bruised cells to regenerate only do so by His perfect order and divine design. The wisdom, skill, and intellect behind medical practices are also ascribed to God, yet no physician can heal your inner man. No doctor can heal your soul wounds. No surgical instrument can reach you as deeply as the Word of God. No magnifying lamp or lighting technology can shine bright enough for any learned professional to dissect the source of your pain and its genealogy. Nothing in you is hidden from God and He is fully equipped to enlighten our darkness without the assistance of unsanctified practice.

Hebrews 4:12 (AMPC) —

> "For the Word that God speaks is alive and full of power [making it active, operative, energizing, and effective]; it is sharper than any two-edged sword, penetrating to the dividing line of the breath of life (soul) and [the immortal] spirit, and of joints and marrow [of the deepest parts of our nature], exposing and sifting and analyzing and judging the very thoughts and purposes of the heart."

It is the Lord's will and responsibility to "bring to light the hidden things of darkness and reveal the counsels of the hearts" in accordance with His Word (1 Corinthians 4:5). He searches our hearts and minds and is intimately familiar with every fiber of our being.

How?

Because this is where He has placed His light in us, right there near the seat of trauma. He sits in the center of our being, clinging to our human spirit. As the Commander of our body's central station, He knows all about us, even the things we bury or avoid exposing. No one knows and no one can reveal the details of your heart's condition like the Holy Spirit. The Revealer doesn't sit across a desk in a lab coat, nor does He sit across the table looking at tarot cards or into a crystal ball. Our Revealer sits on the throne of our hearts, revealing and healing from the inside.

Jesus knew that if we intended to follow Him that we would need not only a Healer but a Comforter. He provides all we need of Him in the planting of the Holy Ghost in the womb of our being. Those that followed lamented over the announcement of Christ's pending crucifixion. They were unaware that His death unlocked the mystery of God's original intention for all mankind which was fellowship in the most intimate way.

After Christ had risen from the dead, Mary Magdalene was found by Jesus as she wept at his empty tomb (John 20:1-13). Can you imagine how relieved she felt after recognizing the voice of the Lord again? Of course, she ran to embrace Him like never before.

John 20:17 (NKJV) —

> *"Jesus said to her, 'Do not cling to Me, for I have not yet ascended to My Father; but go to My brethren and say to them, 'I am ascending to My Father and your Father, and to My God and your God.'"*

When Jesus told her not to cling to Him, He was not rejecting her embrace; He was teaching her the purpose of His temporary assignment to the earth. The part of His Person that Mary needed to embrace was not His physical body but His Spirit that would be planted in hers after Christ's ascension.

John 16:7 (NKJV) —

> *"Nevertheless I tell you the truth. It is to your advantage that I go away; for if I do not go away, the Helper will not come to you; but if I depart, I will send Him to you."*

The physical body of Jesus could not be shared by the world in intimacy. Christ did not appear before man to remain a physical comrade. He came to reveal the hidden mysteries leading us to the chamber of the Father. His sacrifice has given us access that Holy Spirit teaches us to navigate. The veil has been torn that kept man separated from the Most Holy Place, and the red carpet that we call the blood of Jesus now welcomes us in. This mystery is no longer hidden, and as you navigate the expanse of God's presence in your life of worship, more mysteries are soon to be revealed. You are His temple, and He is your heaven. You don't have to travel to build this altar. This altar is not limited to the four walls of any church. This altar is one that you live in daily.

In Christ's encounter with the Samaritan woman in the gospel of John, He shared something paramount to the understanding of every worshiper. She was accustomed to the practice of worship in a particular location.

John 4:20 (NKJV) —

> *"Our fathers worshiped on this mountain, and you Jews say that in Jerusalem is the place where one ought to worship."*

To her point, Jesus remarked:

> *"Jesus said to her, 'Woman, believe Me, the hour is coming when you will neither on this mountain nor in Jerusalem, worship the Father.'"*

The Samaritan woman whose name we do not know was unable to recognize that the Location of worship was standing right in front of her. In the presence of Jesus is where the worshiper worships. He said these words to her:

John 4:23-24 (NKJV) —

> *"But the hour is coming, and now is, when the true worshipers will worship the Father in spirit and truth; for the Father is seeking such to worship Him. God is Spirit, and those who worship Him must worship in spirit and truth."*

We worship God in spirit when we are reborn in spirit. This happens at our new birth or salvation. As Jesus taught Nicodemus in John 3:1-6, our new birth is not natural but spiritual and inducts us into the unseen realm of God's kingdom. "God is Spirit," therefore because He is not limited to any single location (not even heaven), neither is our worship. To worship in truth is to employ our natural faculties and our humanity in submission to His deity as a lifestyle beyond a location.

To worship in truth is to intentionally keep the reality of God in our minds daily. The portal by which we access our heavenly Father is available to us continually but grows in depth and dimension with pursuit. I liken our relationships with Him to that reflecting a couple's established yet flourishing courtship. Worship is not designated to a single place but to a single heart of the ones who love God.

Imagine your romantic interest is away at work or traveling. What keeps you connected exists in the heart and is further established with some degree of a spoken covenant when the relationship was initiated. Physically, you cannot reach them, but they are on your mind and heart daily. The thoughts of your heart provoke communication exchanges throughout the day that aren't moment by moment but leave lasting impressions. What you communicate and how you communicate speaks to the other party that they are in your thoughts. What is spoken from your heart to the other ferments the connection.

This chapter started by mentioning that while you may not always feel near to God, your abiding place in Him and His abiding place in you is permanent. While you may become busy with life, know that His ear is always attentive to hear every utterance of your heart. Whether it be a sighed "Thank You, Lord" or an hour of prayer, He hears you. Keeping your lines of communication open to God is critical to the life of the worshipper.

The intimate expression of worship cultivates a personal chamber where God's ear and His heart hear every word with pleasure. Like He did with

Noah, so He will be soothed by your offering of worship. Most often, we are encouraged to pray and praise. We are led in prayer meetings, and we apply the formula of the Lord's prayer given to us in Matthew 6:9-13. *"Men ought always to pray"* (Luke 18:1 NKJV). A life of worship could never not include prayer because prayer is a power portal. Worship adds passion to prayer, taking you to another dimension. My focus in these last few pages is to develop your love language called worship.

I recently did an exercise with a client intrigued by the discussion of the beauty of worship I was discussing in the salon. I took her through this exercise that I will offer you as a pattern to follow. Using Psalm 23 as our point of scriptural reference, I began teaching her how to pray the Word of God. It was such an amazing thing to feel the tangible presence of God swell in the room as this sweet, innocent, beautiful soul yielded her heart to pray. She shared that she had a prayer life, but she wanted to go deeper and asked me how.

She began to read the Psalms, and every few words I would stop her and ask her to define the words she read as well as gauge her understanding. I did not want her to define the words to me or the others in the space. I wanted her to define the words in prayer, lengthening her 'talk time' with God. This is how Holy Spirit increased my prayer life. This exact method is what He taught me when I would ask to be taken deeper during my earlier months in federal prison. This is how Holy Spirit taught me to pray. When we started, she would say, "Lord, I thank You for being my Shepherd. I thank You for making me not want. Thank You, Father, for making me lie down in green pastures," and so on. Outside of the scripture itself, she added very few words.

I would ask her, "What is a shepherd? Define what you just read in your own words, add your understanding to it, and speak it unto God." This is how your prayer life becomes layered and expanded. Add your understanding of the Word and lift it all up to God. Expand your vocabulary in prayer this way.

She went on to define a shepherd as a leader and as one who takes care of his flock. So, her prayer then became:

"Lord, thank You for being my Shepherd, the one that leads me and guides me. Thank You for taking care of me and watching over me as a shepherd does his flock. Thank You, Father, for providing every need, for keeping me sheltered and safe from danger as a shepherd does his flock. Thank You, Father, for leading me beside waters that are still, where I can find calm, peace, and rest."

It became evident that her understanding was enlightened, and the presence of God began to fill the salon space. After praying through the Psalm, I told her "Now convert your prayer into worship." After explaining, she and everyone in the room understood the assignment. I told her, "I just heard you pray that the Lord is your shepherd. You didn't say that the Lord was the Shepherd of the world, of the city, or your family. You said he was a shepherd over you which makes His leadership extremely personal considering all you've described in prayer."

The scenario I offered was this: Imagine your mate walks into a room of five people with food for everyone to eat. Each person thanks him and appreciates the gesture. What he did was really nice but was done for everyone in the room. It was personally enjoyed but not personally offered. I'm a woman, so I will relate it from this angle. Now imagine that same mate sending you love notes throughout the day as well as an invitation to a five-course meal at a five-star restaurant at 7:00 pm. He has a courier deliver you a dress and a pair of stilettos from one of Neiman Marcus' newest collections, all of which fits to a T. When you arrive home from work, you see that he has placed rose petals from the front door to the bedroom closet where you see your new items hung. He knows what time you get in, and in anticipation of you experiencing his outpour of love follows with another text saying: Be ready by 6:00. At around 5:58 pm, you peer through your bedroom window only to find a black sedan outside with a driver standing by the open rear passenger door. On the dot, the door rings, and on the other side stands your knight in shining armor, having lavished you with love all day long. When you open the door, what will you do? What will you say? How will you feel? How will you express your gratitude?

That response is a type of worship. Your "thank you" will come with affection. Your gratitude is seasoned with deep passion. Your reflection is one of intimacy, not surface or empty at all. The extravagance in your response to this dream date is likened to worship of the Lord your God. Worship identifies the individual attention, care, and love released by God over you. Your sensitivity to how specific every characteristic of God toward you will provoke an intimacy in you creating a cloud of worship. Worship is passionate, extravagant communication from your heart to God's in consideration of all He has done for us. When you consider His acts to be personal and specific to your every need, the impact is much deeper. When you communicate that consideration unto God, it creates the most beautiful worship.

Like my client using Psalm 23, make the work of the Shepherd personal and release that personal expression out loud. That morning, in my salon space, we went around the room, each taking a portion of this Psalm and converting it into worship.

> *"Father, in the name of Jesus, thank You that You cover me, keep me, protect me, guide me, and steer me into paths that keep my safety and mind. You are such a good Father to me, and I love and appreciate You for Your consistency. Never have I been led astray by You who guides me only into truth. Lord, You are the answer to every need that I could ever have before I need it. As a shepherd tends to his flock with every detail of each sheep in mind, oh God, so do You care for me. You are*

faithful to provide all of my needs according to Your riches and glory, and You deny me nothing.

Therefore, in You, Abba Father, I shall not want, not now, not tomorrow, not next year, not ever.

Thank You, Father. Thank You, Lord. Thank You, Jehovah. I love You, God, with a tremendous love. You are my King, and You are forever seated on the throne of my heart.

I lift up holy hands without wrath and doubt, understanding that You withhold no good thing from those that love You. Everything good in my life, You author; therefore, I am not in need, and if I were, You would supply it before I ask.

You give me rest beside still waters where Your peace that knows no end is mine. Your everlasting peace is my portion forever, oh God. Jesus, You give me peace that surpasses all understanding, and in Your peace, I find rest for my weary soul. Lord, I rest in You for You, God, are my hope of glory. You are the reason that my head can be lifted high. You remind me of my expected end. My hope is in You; therefore, I trust You with all of me forever."

This could go on forever. A worshipper's heart takes the acts of God personally, and once the river of worship begins to flow, it can become unstoppable.

I always encourage people to add soaking instrumental worship to the atmosphere when wanting to spend time in worship. Music of any kind bypasses the mind and goes right into the soul that needs to be stilled for worship. With words or by sitting in silence, you will find great refreshment in this place. Worship is your secret place. It is your hiding place of shelter. In worship, your eyes will be opened to God but blinded to fallen enemies, for in this place, your defense is the shadow of His wings.

Find rest in this place. Surrender there. See God bigger than anything going on in your life at the moment. When you see Him high and lifted up above the circumstances of your life, you make room for His greatness to manifest in every place, rendering your wholeness complete.

When you worship, you don't have to spend time trying to find God. When you worship, God looks for you.

Made in the USA
Middletown, DE
02 May 2022

65120826R00071